THE TRAGIC PROTEST

DAVID ANDERSON

The Tragic Protest

*A Christian study of some
modern literature*

SCM PRESS LTD
LONDON

334 01685 1

First published 1969
by SCM Press Ltd
56 Bloomsbury Street London WC1

© SCM Press Ltd 1969

Printed in Great Britain by
Northumberland Press Limited
Gateshead

To
The Staff and Students
of
Wycliffe Hall, Oxford
1962-1968

Contents

Acknowledgements

I gratefully acknowledge permission of authors, publishers, and other copyright holders to quote from the following books:

Wolfgang Borchert, *Draussen vor der Tür*, Rowohlt Verlag, Hamburg

Albert Camus, *The Plague, The Rebel, The Fall*, Hamish Hamilton Ltd and Alfred A. Knopf, Inc.

Nigel Dennis, *Cards of Identity*, Weidenfeld & Nicolson Ltd and Vanguard Press, Inc.

T. S. Eliot, *The Waste Land, The Dry Salvages*, Faber and Faber Ltd and Harcourt, Brace and World, Inc.

W. Golding, *Lord of the Flies*, Faber and Faber Ltd and Coward-McCann

W. Golding, *The Spire*, Faber and Faber Ltd and Harcourt, Brace and World, Inc.

Erich Heller, *The Disinherited Mind*, Bowes and Bowes Ltd

R. Kipling, *Sussex*, from the Definitive Edition of Rudyard Kipling's Verse, Mrs George Bambridge, The Macmillan Co. and Doubleday and Company, Inc.

A. Koestler, *The Invisible Writing*, Hamilton and Collins Ltd and The Macmillan Co.

Charles Moeller, *Littérature du XXe siècle et christianisme*, Casterman S.A. Editeurs

L. Mumford, *The Condition of Man*, Martin Secker and Warburg Ltd and Harcourt, Brace and World, Inc.

F. Nietzsche, *Thus Spake Zarathustra*, tr. R. J. Hollingdale, Penguin Books Ltd

Elimo P. Njau, *African Art*, The First International Congress of Africanists, Longmans Green & Co.

Camille Roussan, *Christ*, The First International Congress of Africanists, Longmans Green & Co.

J.-P. Sartre, *The Reprieve, Iron in the Soul (Troubled Sleep)*, Hamish Hamilton Ltd and Alfred A. Knopf, Inc.

J.-P. Sartre, *Situations III*, Editions Gallimard

Ignazio Silone, *The Choice of Comrades*, Encounter Ltd

H. Thielicke, *Nihilism*, Routledge and Kegan Paul Ltd and Harper and Row, Inc.

Philip Thody, *Albert Camus 1913-1960*, Hamish Hamilton Ltd and The Macmillan Company

Angus Wilson, *Albert Camus*, N.R.F. ler mars 1960, Editions Gallimard

Preface

This book is based on lectures given in the Faculty of Theology at Oxford in 1964 and 1966, though the material has undergone something of a metamorphosis in course of writing. I have benefited from discussion with those who attended the lectures and also from critical scrutiny of my interpretations by College and University Societies, the Modern Churchmen's Union, and the American Summer School at Mansfield College. I wish to thank the Principal of Mansfield, Dr John Marsh, for inviting me to lecture to the Summer School in three successive years.

The inscription records a special debt to my own colleagues and students, who have heard a good deal of the material in one way or another and whose comments have urged me to think harder. The skill of the students in interpreting contemporary literature was recently demonstrated by a performance of *Waiting for Godot* given in Wycliffe chapel.

I am grateful to personal friends who have encouraged me: Dr Max Warren, who suggested that I should read a paper to the Evangelical Fellowship for Theological Literature in 1958; Dr F. W. Dillistone, whose knowledge of this field is equalled only by his generosity in sharing it; and Professor Douglas Webster, whose alertness and industry during a two-year sojourn at Wycliffe often reproached my lassitude.

My secretary, Miss Carol Jackson, has cheerfully shouldered extra burdens during my work on this book and has also typed the manuscript. My wife has either urged me on or resisted my obsession according to the need of the moment, and my children have accepted my frequent disappearances into my study.

My indebtedness to other writers is evident in the text and notes. I should like to make particular mention of Charles Moeller's vast work, *Littérature du XXe siècle et christianisme*, to which I have often turned.

This book has not been one of those that write themselves – if any books are. Apart from my own ignorance, the main difficulty has been that of construction. It has been hard to connect up the diverse literary material into a unified whole while at the same time avoiding the distortions that would result from forcing everything into a pre-empted scheme. Nevertheless, the book is meant to be read as a unity and not as a collection of separate pieces: thus the reader will find that a discussion in one chapter is taken up elsewhere in a different context and in relation to the work of another writer. The unity of the book is formed by persisting themes which, I hope, are elicited from the material and are not imposed upon it.

I also hope that I have been at least partly successful in avoiding the temptation to use literature merely as a new wineskin for the old Christian wine. I do not care for those books which try to show that writers who reject Christianity are really Christians in spite of themselves. I prefer to say that the writers selected here have deepened and extended my awareness of what it means to be a human being, and that in so doing they have raised questions about humanness concerning which Christianity has some comments to make and some explanations to offer. But this does not mean that there are Christian answers as it were waiting fully armed in the wings, determined to rush on to the stage whether or not they receive the appropriate cue. The human drama changes, and if the Christian part to be played in it is to avoid *unnecessary* oddity, it must at least get its emphases right. I have tried to pick out a few of the themes present in the drama which is being written for our time and to suggest the sort of lines which may be suitable for the Christian part in it. The reader will doubtless decide for himself whether that part is of a Hamlet-like importance or of an Osric-like triviality. By conviction as well as profession, I am a Prince of Denmark man.

More accurately, the drama is the one which I think is being written. There is no way of concealing this personal factor. It appears in the choice of authors – why these rather than others? – and in the selective use I have made of their work. I am most conscious of this selectiveness – amounting perhaps to distortion – in my treatment of Sartre, whose complexities are sufficiently well known. But to write a book of this kind it is necessary both to limit the field and to determine at least the general direction of the course. The reader who desires a thorough treatment of the writers whose work I have discussed can easily refer to the specialists. One may instance Anthony Manser on Sartre, Philip Thody on Camus, Kinkead-Weekes and Gregor on Golding, and so on. My own concern has been to explore a small area of what in the first chapter I have called 'the context of feeling', and to apply the result, as a 'critique of satisfaction', to Christian theology.

I have included a chapter on African novels, partly in memory of six happy years as a C.M.S. missionary at Immanuel College in Nigeria, but more importantly as a small recognition of the fact that there are other literatures, other versions of the human drama, besides those of Europe and America.

I think this book will be intelligible to those who have read few or even none of the novels to which I refer, but it is obvious that those who *have* read them will be far better able to weigh my discussion than those who have not. They are all available in English in paperback editions. Many are in the invaluable series of Modern Classics published by Penguin Books.

I am aware that a book which makes a modest attempt to bring together literature and theology is likely to be viewed with suspicion by the professionals on both sides. Literary men dislike having the mines of literature salted with theological ideas, and there are probably still some theologians who think that the queen of the sciences is an absolute monarch. Both parties may find comfort in the following quotation from Nigel Dennis's *Cards of Identity* (Penguin Books, p. 146), with which I have sometimes ended my lectures.

> How we love the beginnings of orations – the expectant silence, the promise, so rarely kept, of novelty! But how much more we love orations' ends! Like prisoners at last released, we wander

free in the world of our own thoughts. We see the speaker resume his seat, and as his last words fade into the past, never to be recalled, we start forward in our chairs, burning to press on him, in the disguise of questions, the ideas with which we have consoled ourselves throughout his address. We applaud him not because he has brought his own history to a close but because he has at last brought our own closer to a beginning.

Wycliffe Hall, Oxford,
Michaelmas 1968

I

The Human Context

Mankind today is in poor shape. Any portrait of modern man,
if at all faithful to the original, cannot but be deformed, split,
fragmentary – in a word, tragic.

The Italian novelist Ignazio Silone wrote those words in 1954,[1]
and they seemed to sum up the feeling of shock and outrage
which perhaps the majority of Europeans – and others – were
still experiencing in the aftermath of war. We knew that we
had been contemporaries of the worst tyranny and the greatest
mass-extermination in history. We knew that appalling mush-
rooms had grown in the sky. We knew that we had witnessed,
and indeed shared in, a devaluation of man which seemed to
have put every ideology in question. It looked as if the human
estimate would have to be reconstructed from the foundation
up. For many, it had become utterly impossible to subscribe to
the old optimistic prognosis of Man. François Mauriac was only
one of those who believed that the doctrine of rational progressivism had been totally demolished.

> Here, he wrote, is the moment of history at which all the potions
> with which hope has intoxicated itself are revealing themselves,
> at one and the same time, as poisons. The foolish hope which,
> in 1789, set out to conquer happiness . . . this foolish hope which
> rushed headlong along so many routes, following the Jacobins
> and the worshippers of the deified nation, following the double
> posterity of Voltaire and Jean-Jacques, following the Saint-Simon-
> ians, the ideologues of 1848, following those who believed in the
> infinite progress of the enlightened – this poor hope discovers
> today that all these routes converge on the same concentration
> camp, on the same gas chamber, on the debris of bombed towns,
> on the atrociously burnt corpses of Hiroshima.[2]

Other post-war writers expressed a similar sense of devastation. We are like refugees without papers. We are all in the condemned cell. We are camping in the ruins of the world. Society has been atomized . . . As Koestler said, it seemed shameful to be alive. What possible estimate of man could even begin to encompass the degradation which humanity had suffered and inflicted? Could we revert to our old doctrines and discount recent events as the result of a temporary aberration? Could we still be democrats or humanists or Marxists or Christians and carry on as though nothing very serious had happened? Or had we reached a kind of zero-point from which it would be necessary to rethink our anthropologies?

Much of the literature, the novels and plays, of this post-war period conveyed a sense of isolation and futility. God himself seemed to have abdicated, and had certainly been remarkably silent and inactive during the travail of man in the twentieth century. A German poet, Wolfgang Borchert, wrote a play which he called *Draussen vor der Tür* (Outside the Door) in which God appeared in the guise of a weeping old man wringing his hands helplessly over the sufferings and follies of the human race.

'I can do nothing,' says God. 'Just so,' Beckmann replies, 'you can do nothing. We do not fear you any more. We do not love you any more. You are not modern. The theologians have let you become an old man . . . You speak low at present, too low for the thunder of our time. We cannot hear you any more . . . Perhaps you have too much ink in your blood, the fluid ink of the theologians. They have shut you up in the churches, we cannot hear each other any more . . .'[3]

The play ends with the words:

'Why are you silent then? Why? Is there no reply then? No reply at all?'

The hero of this play, Beckmann, is a German soldier, a survivor of Stalingrad as was Borchert himself. He represents the persistence in mind and soul of the outrage of war which everyone else is determined as quickly as possible to forget. He applies for a job in a cabaret but is repulsed because he is still wearing his army spectacles. There is no place for Beckmann in the post-war world. He is the man *outside the door*, incapable of sharing in the make-believe of a return to 'normal' life and convinced that even God has had to admit that humanity is now beyond him.

Not everyone felt the discovery of God's weakness in the modern world as poignantly as Borchert, and there were those who rejoiced that at last man had become free to grapple with the realities of his existence without supernatural aid. But in any case there was obviously a lot of theological rethinking to be done, a lot of old ink to be washed out of the divine system, if faith were to become possible again. It had become necessary, in Bonhoeffer's well-known phrase, to speak in 'a secular fashion' of God, to offer some credible doctrine of his presence in the world in spite of his notorious absence from it. The long perspectives and *ab extra* interventions associated with metaphysical theism were not only hard to believe: they were also largely irrelevant to men and women who were faced with an immense task of reconstruction and whose attention was wholly fixed on the here and now. Much theological writing since the war has therefore been concerned to present God as one who is active in the world, not as a *deus ex machina*, but as a participant in the pains and travails of human life – the God revealed in the incarnate Christ as the lover and the servant of men who is always being edged out into the wilderness and on to a cross. The weakness of God in the world has been understood, not as a defect fatal to theism, but as the central saving truth of the Gospel of Jesus Christ. The silence of God amid the outrages of our century has compelled us to realize afresh that the God of the Gospel is disclosed, not in arbitrary superventions of power, but by the participation of the Crucified in the forsakenness of man.

To those who were under the impression that religion is about man's dependence upon a supernatural Power, this doctrine of the weakness of God has seemed hardly distinguishable from atheism. But if the God upon whom we depend is thought to be one who negates human responsibility and freedom by accommodating the world to a metaphysical blueprint laid down in advance, then it is clear that Christianity is and always has been atheistic in this sense. The New Testament does not understand divine power in terms of coercive authority. In the New Testament we see that the triumphant God is the *suffering* God, not the detached, impassible 'God of the philosophers' who imposes his own prefabricated paradigms on human life from the outside. At the same time, however, we see that the God disclosed to us in Christ is not so completely absorbed into the human context as to be indistinguishable from it. God has not nihilated himself in the world; he has not ceased to be transcendent. The New Testament witnesses to a God who participates in human life in order to affirm and fulfil it, and whose love has the power to create that which it desires to find.

Another charge of atheism is made against theologians when they try to translate the Christian confession of faith into contemporary human terms. Alasdair MacIntyre has argued that this procedure is 'doomed to one of two failures'. Either the theologians succeed in their translation: 'in which case what they find themselves saying has been transformed into the atheism of their hearers. Or they fail in their translation: in which case no one hears what they have to say but themselves'.[4] One or other of these failures may indeed be inevitable if theology starts, as MacIntyre assumes it does, with the transcendent, wholly – other God of metaphysical theism. They need not occur if one begins with Jesus Christ in whom the divine and the human are united. When we begin with him, we realize that we do not have to 'translate' God into human terms; God has himself already done this in Christ, and our job is more like one of appending footnotes to the translation. To take the Incarnation seriously is to see that nothing human – perhaps not even atheism – is alien to the God revealed to us in Christ.

The answer of Paul Tillich to the kind of dilemma posed by MacIntyre was to say that existential questions and theological answers exist 'in correlation'.[5] The answers are not derived from the questions but are *elicited* by them and find their relevance in them. Theology simply fails to communicate anything when it ignores the questions which actually shape themselves in human life. But this does not mean that theology is merely a disguised anthropology: the method of correlation maintains the dialectic of 'the divine-human encounter'. 'The decisive aspect of theology,' says Tillich, 'is its incarnational and existential aspect.' This is seen in the God-manhood of Christ; it is also seen in man's immediate experience of his own existence.

Tillich's method of correlation has been expressed by Paul Lehmann in terms of what he calls 'contextual' theology.[6] He points out that theology cannot ignore the positivistic emphasis which is taken for granted nowadays in the secular disciplines. This means that theologians must carefully notice the actual conditions in which they 'do' theology – the human realities disclosed in the contexts of contemporary life. Such a contextual approach to theology, says Lehmann, 'resolves itself into the task of translating the language and conceptions of the tradition into their *human* reality and meaning'. The ultimate test of this humanizing responsibility of theology 'may well be its hospitality to what it can learn about the genuinely human from other perspectives . . .' In other words, theology can be contextual only if those who write it make some attempt to understand the context to which they address themselves and in which the 'existential questions' arise.

I have suggested that it may be misleading to think of the theological task as one of 'translation'. The Christian 'tradition' of which Lehmann speaks, however, does not begin with a set of metaphysical theistic concepts having no correlatives in the human context: it begins with the divine-human reality of Jesus Christ. The theologian is therefore more like someone who edits a book for a new edition – not rewriting the text, but adding explanatory comments, supplying modern illustrations in place of outdated ones, relating the author's insights to immediate situations, and so on. We do not have to humanize God: it would be nearer the truth to say that we have to understand our own humanity in terms of his. This is the sense in which theology has to be 'contextual': it is a matter of relating what is 'genuinely human' in man to the God-manhood of Christ.

The human context of which Lehmann speaks may be divided, for convenience only, into the context of knowledge and the context of feeling and ideas. So far as the context of knowledge is concerned, theology has painfully discovered that Cartesian dualism is theologically disastrous, and it has taken account, though often with notorious reluctance, of discovered scientific truth. At present, it seems to be the comparatively new disciplines of sociology, psychology and anthropology that are claiming the greatest theological attention, though it looks as if biological studies are beginning to rival them in importance. But far less attention is paid to the context of *feeling*. What do men hope for? What would they die for? What rouses them to protest? What causes them to tremble? If theology is to be 'contextual', I believe it must address itself to the ways in which *these* questions are answered in the contemporary world as well as to the data which emerge from scientific and philosophical investigation.

A good many years ago, T. E. Hulme raised the question of what he called 'a critique of satisfaction'.[7] On what grounds does the philosopher claim that his picture of man's relationship to the world is a *satisfying* picture? Hulme argued that the humanistic 'canons of satisfaction' which, he believed, had prevailed among European philosophers since the Renaissance, had been accepted *uncritically*, and had produced shallow conceptions of the nature and destiny of man. No world-view, however awe-inspiringly the arguments for it may be presented, can be satisfying if it fails to match the range and depth of man's interior vision. Hulme thought that the humanistic canons of satisfaction, unconsciously held, were trivial and inadequate and ought to be subjected to a critique.* I suggest that the canons of *theological* satisfaction will equally fail to satisfy contemporary man, however well argued the theological case may be, if they are, in Hulme's words, merely 'the reverence for tradition, the desire to recapture the sentiment of Fra Angelico'. A critique of *these* canons is also needed. I think that such a critique will mainly be derived from what I have rather vaguely

---

* An attempt at such a critique has been made in *Objections to Humanism*, ed. by Blackham, Constable & Co., 1963 and Penguin Books. See also R. Bambrough's essay, 'Praising with Faint Damns' in *Religion and Humanism*, BBC Publications.

called 'the context of feeling'. What we have to ask as we set about writing our footnotes to the Gospel is whether we can give some account of what it is like to be a human being in the twentieth century. Can we analyse and set out the context of feeling?

Apart from what we may discover by introspection, the main sources of the context of feeling are the arts. What we have in artistic creation is an expression of how sensitive men and women of a particular age feel about themselves and their world. Of course there is no simple, consistent picture. Attempts at clarification can do no more than point to emphases and recurrences; definitions will always fail to do justice to the complexities and will therefore be false. I am not oblivious to the fact that art can reach a level of greatness at which it speaks to men of every age, but I wish to claim that there are some special emphases in modern art – though I shall confine my attention to literature – which speak to me not as a human being in some timeless sense but as a human being of *this* century. To borrow Gerhard Ebeling's distinction, modern literature raises questions in which I appear personally even though I am not specifically mentioned, and I feel myself to be in some measure responsible for the answers that are given.[8] These questions are distinguishable from others – those with which the sciences are concerned – in which I am *not* included, and indeed *must* not be included if the answers are to be 'objective'.* Art raises what we may call the 'I' questions to which theology must attend if its contemporary witness is to be 'contextual'.

Modern literature is vast and multi-dimensional. A selection from it must therefore be made which can hardly claim to be founded on anything more cogent than personal knowledge and taste. But what assurance is there that the tiny proportion of literature selected for treatment really does give us a picture of what is 'genuinely human' in the second half of the twentieth century? I am afraid the answer to this question must lie with

* Though Arthur Koestler, among others, has shown what an enormous part is played in scientific discovery by apparently subjective factors. See *The Act of Creation*, Hutchinson, London 1964 and Pan Books, 1966.

the individual reader. If he has found that the writers mentioned here have raised for him the 'I' questions of which we have spoken, well and good. But if they have not, then he will have to make his own selection and write his own book.

I myself am unable to subscribe to the view of some that literature which was influenced by the events of 1939-45 can now be dismissed as a product of a kind of war-neurosis with nothing to say to us in normal conditions. I agree with Borchert that conditions can never be 'normal' again after collapse on such a scale. Angus Wilson made this point when he wrote about Albert Camus after the latter's death in 1960 and said that English humanists were tempted to regard the work of Camus as a study of the abnormal and exceptional with little meaning for ordinary life. 'The thought of Camus', Wilson wrote, 'concerning the evil in humanity, useless suffering, sorrow without hope, seems to them (the English humanists) forced, and dangerously near the emotive frontier where humanity slides towards Christianity.'[9] While it is of course true that the apocalyptic experiences presented by Camus are 'abnormal', nevertheless they have a habit of revealing the deceptiveness of the structures of normality. The terrible puzzles of human existence can be ignored in times of ease and complacency; but like the plague in Camus's novel, they bide their time, hidden perhaps but not nullified.

I wish to assert, with Berdyaev, that great changes have taken place in the European soul, and that the major writers referred to in this book have disclosed elements in human self-awareness which, if not wholly new, at least are felt with a new intensity. Berdyaev remarks that the disclosure may be said to have begun, 'not in the twentieth but in the nineteenth century – in the Romantics, Kierkegaard, Dostoevsky, Nietzsche, the Symbolists'.[10] It may even have begun in Hamlet, who was as much aware of the absence of essences as any modern Existentialist. I have attempted to indicate the nature of this disclosure in my title – The Tragic Protest – by which I mean to draw attention to what I believe to be two of its main components.

First is the emphasis upon the value and finality of the unrepeatable human individual and the deepened awareness of the forces in modern life which deny and threaten this value and this finality. If I can no longer feel that my selfhood is supported and even in part created by my participation in accepted social, cultural and ideological orders; if, in fact, I have come to the conclusion that such participation leads in the end to a *denial* of my selfhood: then I quickly discover that I am affirmed by nothing, and I find in myself the kind of anxiety which seems to be most appropriately described by such terms as non-being, despair, alienation, and the like. Most of the writers I have selected are concerned to press upon us the reality and significance of such experience, and to detach us from the structures we erect on the surface of life in order to conceal our fundamentally *unsupported* existence. They are therefore 'tragic' writers, and they are so in the deepest sense because they question not merely the external conditions of our life, which there is always the hope of improving, but the very meaning of human existence itself. I am using the word 'tragic' in my title in this sense – the sense in which Silone uses it in the quotation at the beginning of this chapter.

The other word – 'protest' – has perhaps become somewhat over-familiar recently. It puts us in mind of civil rights marchers, student demonstrators, and the whole phenomenon of protest which has become a characteristic of our time and has already brought one government to the verge of collapse. I believe that the roots of this powerful growth are to be found in modern literature of the kind which perhaps originated in the novels and stories of Kafka just after the first war. Such literature has been prophetic, in the sense that it has not merely diagnosed a tendency of our time but has promoted and activated it – to an extent which, one suspects, now astonishes some of its creators. This literature has itself been called the literature of protest, and one of the things against which it has been protesting is admirably set out in the following passage from Camus's novel *The Fall*:

Power . . . settles everything. It took time, but we finally realized that. For instance, you must have noticed that our old Europe at last philosophizes in the right way. We no longer say as in simple times: 'This is my opinion. What are your objections?' We have become lucid. For the dialogue we have substituted the communiqué. 'This is the truth,' we say. 'You can discuss it as

much as you want; we aren't interested. But in a few years there'll
be the police to show you I'm right.'[11]

It could be argued that demonstrations are not obviously im-
provements on communiqués: truth tends to be a casualty of
both procedures. Demonstrations, particularly violent ones, do
not always lead to dialogue, and the pulling down of existing
structures may not advance the cause of freedom if only chaos
is left. There is, in fact, a deeper, a more basic protest than that
which is directed against social and political structures. It is
the protest against the fundamental alienation of man from
any order which is capable of affirming his personal being. This
'tragic' protest, I believe, underlies other forms of protest and
may partly account for the element of irrationality and violence
in them. In the deepest recess of our being we know that no
human structure is so absolutely final as to be worthy of our
total commitment. At the same time, therefore, we know that
nothing in the human order is capable of guaranteeing the
reality of selfhood without which our final state can only be
one of despair. The tragic protest is the discovery that the world
provides no correlate which is adequate to the range and depth
of our interior dream. It is therefore tragic in another sense –
that it does not succeed in alleviating our despair.

These are the senses in which the contemporary, human
meaning of the title of this book is to be understood. But I hope
to show that it also has a *theological* meaning which is 'correla-
tive' to the human one and finds its anchorage in the divine-
human Protest of Jesus Christ. I shall claim that it is only
when the human protest is incorporated into *his* Protest that it
ceases to lose itself in a void.

To revert to Lehmann's terminology, we can say that we are
shifting the tragic protest from its human context to its divine
context. Or rather, lest we give the impression that we are, after
all, leaving the 'human' behind, it would be better to say that we
are *extending* the context into the divine. This extension is, of
course, presumptuous and impossible if we think of the divine
in terms of metaphysical theism, which necessarily *excludes*
the human. But it becomes perfectly possible if we think in terms
of Jesus Christ, in whom God-manhood is already a reality.

Karl Barth has said that it is 'when we look at Jesus that we know decisively that God's deity does not exclude, but includes his humanity'. In Jesus Christ, God encounters us as Man as well as God, and he encounters us as one who 'takes to his heart the weakness and the perversity, the helplessness and the misery, of the human race surrounding him'.[12] There is, we may believe, nothing which the humanity of Jesus excludes – nothing human is alien to him who was Son of Man. Whatever he did not experience directly, he knew through his complete openness to others. Jesus was wholly vulnerable to the joys and sorrows, the failures and the hopes of the world of men. That is why, from one aspect, he was weak and helpless in the world. But it is his vulnerability, which is part of the meaning of love, that qualifies him to be the Saviour of the world.

Yet vulnerability to man's condition is useless if it is not accompanied by power to change that condition. Because Jesus is Son of God as well as Son of Man, he is able to take the human context, which is marked by alienation and death, into the divine context, which is marked by affirmation and resurrection. It is love, not pity, that recreates. In Jesus Christ the tragic protest of man becomes the creative Protest of God.

Notes

1. Ignazio Silone, 'The Choice of Comrades' in *Encounter*, December 1954.

2. Quoted by Charles Moeller, *Littérature du XXe siècle et christianisme*, Tome III, Casterman, Paris 1957, p. 425.

3. Wolfgang Borchert, *Draussen vor der Tür*, Harrap, London 1963, p. 123.

4. A. MacIntyre, 'God and the Theologians' in *Encounter*, September 1963.

5. P. Tillich, *Systematic Theology Vol. I*, James Nisbet, Welwyn Garden City 1953, p. 67f. and University of Chicago Press, 1951.

6. P. Lehmann, 'On Doing Theology' in *Prospect for Theology*, ed. Healey, James Nisbet, Welwyn Garden City 1966.

7. T. E. Hulme, *Speculations*, Routledge & Kegan Paul, London 1936, pp. 16-23.

8. Gerhard Ebeling, *The Nature of Faith*, Collins Fontana Books, London 1961 and Muhlenberg Press, Philadelphia 1962.

9. Angus Wilson's article appeared in *La Nouvelle Revue Française, Hommage à Albert Camus*, March 1960.

10. N. Berdyaev, *The Divine and the Human*, Geoffrey Bles, London 1949, pp. 55-56 and the Macmillan Co., New York 1949.

11. A. Camus, *The Fall*, Hamish Hamilton, London 1957, Penguin Books 1963, p. 35 and Alfred A. Knopf, New York 1957.

12. K. Barth, *The Humanity of God*, Collins, London 1961, pp. 49-51 and John Knox Press, Richmond 1966.

2

Man at Absolute Zero

The most vigorous and uncompromising celebrant of the tragic protest since the war has undoubtedly been the French philosopher and writer, Jean-Paul Sartre. He has said that it is the writer's job 'to pose problems in the most radical and intransigent manner' and to revolt 'against everything "inculcated" that one may have within oneself'.[1] No one could say that Sartre has not done precisely this in his own work. He is our great demolition expert for whom the only possible starting-point is zero; and his influence, not merely in Europe, has been tremendous.

Sartre's existentialism spoke in the post-war years to people who were sick of being pushed around by ideological fanatics and imperialists. After the European experience of collectivist treatment under the 'apparatus', of occupation, deportation, tortures, imprisonments, and arbitrary executions, people had had enough. The Sartrian ideal of 'authentic existence' was an assertion of individual freedom and responsibility in extreme form. For years, men and women had had to 'appear' in roles dictated by others – the Gestapo, the occupying Power, the State itself. The famous dictum of Sartre, 'Hell is other people', had an unmistakable meaning for those who had endured occupation or militarism. Sartre demanded personal autonomy, the repudiation of every action which is a response to the tyranny of society or of individuals. And he also demanded commitment to the cause of personal freedom, and to the alleviation of physical need without which freedom is impossible.

The protest of Sartre was not directed only against political and social pressures: it is even more important that we should not allow ourselves to be pushed around by the bogus certitudes of doctrine, which are equally and more insidiously capable of depriving us of freedom. The only doctrine about Man is that there is no doctrine – or none which provides him with a model for imitation. Human freedom means freedom from everything, and it therefore begins with a sense of despair and anxiety. We reach despair when we realize that our existence is basically 'absurd' because there are no meanings other than those we ourselves create. We have to fight all the time against the drag towards 'non-being', for there is nothing either in the world or out of it to support our selfhood. Freedom, in fact, is 'terror'.

Sartrianism was not intentionally a philosophy of despair, though it was commonly understood so. It did not merely *accept* the fact that the old ideologies had proved incapable of explaining and supporting the realities of human existence: it claimed that the elimination of those ideologies meant that at last men could address themselves to the challenges of life in a quite new and radical way – a way which had been impossible so long as they had believed themselves to be subject to occult processes. Sartre was not afraid to say that life in many of its aspects *must* be unmeaning and that no permanent values can ever be created. We must learn to live in a state of negativity and doubt, recognizing that this is a mark of the freedom which alone entitles us to call ourselves men. Karl Jaspers summarized this basic conviction when he said, 'Through my experience of Nothingness, indeed inspired only by this extreme experience, I once again, with new faith, sail into the open.'[2]

An early work of Sartre entitled *L'Imagination* shows him to have been strongly affected by the theories of Husserl: 'We know at present', he said, 'that we must start again from zero, neglecting all prephenomenological literature . . .'.[3] More important, however, was the influence of Heidegger, whose difficult 'existentialist' book *Sein und Zeit*[4] had appeared in 1927. There is some evidence that Sartre at first disliked being called an existentialist because he considered that his own teaching differed from that of Heidegger in important ways. In any case, Sartre did what Heidegger could never have done: he presented his own brand of existentialism through the medium of novels and plays which were able to reach a far wider public than was possible for difficult theoretical works, and in so doing he turned his philosophy into a popular movement. This procedure was entirely in accord with existential philosophy itself, which claimed that it did not offer yet another scheme of abstract metaphysics but rather an analysis of what it means to be an individual human being 'thrown' into a specific situation in the world. Sartre was clearly right in thinking that the most effective way of presenting this analysis was by constructing stories about life-situations in which there were *dramatis personae* grappling with specific realities in the contemporary world.

His first novel, *La Nausée*, had actually come out before the war, but already the fundamentals of Sartrianism are manifest in it.[5] The hero of the novel is called Roquentin. He has spent a good many years in various parts of the world, but now, in middle life, he has settled in a French coastal town and is writing a book. But Roquentin is not greatly interested in the eighteenth-century roué whose life he is supposed to be investigating. He is more interested in himself and in the diary to which he confides his thoughts. He feels that he is coming towards the end of a pilgrimage of self-discovery. 'I should like', he says, 'to understand myself before it is too late.'

Roquentin lives alone. He has a few acquaintances in the town: the woman at the café lets him sleep with her from time to time, and there is an odd character whom he nicknames 'l'Autodidacte' who is reading through all the books in the municipal library in alphabetical order. But generally Roquentin goes for solitary walks or stays alone in his room. What he is trying to discover is the nature of the *nausea* which sweeps over him at unexpected moments. It makes him want to vomit, but he knows that the feeling is not basically physical; it has something to do with his own self, his inner reality, and to understand nausea will therefore be to understand himself. Gradually the sense of nausea seems to become permanent: 'it is no longer an illness or a passing fit. It is myself'.

One evening, Roquentin is sitting on a bench in the municipal park. He is looking at the root of a chestnut-tree – a black, knotty, crude mass – when suddenly he is seized by the *existence* of things which presents itself to him as soft, monstrous masses in

disorder – naked, with a frightening, obscene nakedness. Existence brings with it a sense of shame: we feel like apologizing
for it, because the embarrassing thing is that none of us has
the slightest reason for being there; each existent feels superfluous in relation to others. Underneath the hard outline which
presents itself for observation there is only a kind of shapeless,
senseless mass. And this, Roquentin realizes, is true of *all* exist-
ents, including himself. 'I too,' he says, 'was superfluous,' and he
would be superfluous for all time. Roquentin's experience is
a refutation of the Cartesian *cogito*: so far from proving that I
exist, doubt makes me aware of my own inescapable contingency. The key to nausea can be found in one word – Absurdity.
'No necessary being can explain existence: contingency is not
an illusion, an appearance which can be dissipated. It is absolute,
and consequently perfect gratuitousness. Everything is gratuitous, that park, this town, and myself.'

Is it possible, then, to justify one's existence? Is it possible
to accept oneself, to recall one's life without repugnance? These
are the questions Roquentin is asking himself as he waits for the
train to take him back to Paris. Having discovered the nature
of his *nausea*, he will now leave Bouville and start to live at the
level of personal decision, separating out his individual existence
from the monstrous mass of being which has no power of self-
definition.

These thoughts have been prompted by a record being played
in the café as he sits there one evening.

> Some of these days,
> You'll miss me honey.

The man who wrote that song and the negress who sings it have
created something hard and definite, something that 'saves them
from drowning in existence' and by which 'they have cleansed
themselves from the sin of existing'. And perhaps he, Roquentin, may be able to do the same. A book, perhaps, and 'it would
have to be beautiful and hard as steel and make people ashamed
of their existence'. People who read it would think of him as he
thought about the negress. It would define his life and might
even shed some light over his meaningless past so that he might

succeed in accepting himself. So Roquentin makes his way to the station and we leave him there waiting for his train to Paris.

2

La Nausée was published in 1938, and the sense it conveyed of the unreality of existence was very much at variance with the confident political dogmas which were being drummed up at the time. As Anthony Manser points out, it is a highly complex work containing many philosophical subtleties which can easily be missed because of the human, experiential setting of the argument.[6] *La Nausée* is a concentrated, knotted kind of book. There is nothing much in the way of a plot – no development of situations and no ripening of human relationships. But this is deliberate, for Sartre wishes to show, among other things, the banal routine of everyday life in which people conceal from themselves the basic absurdity of their existence. Nothing meaningful will ever happen to the citizens of Bouville: they will forever continue to go to work, to sit in cafés, to discuss trivialities, and to believe in the permanence of human structures. The development of the novel is in the deepening of Roquentin's nausea and his analysis of the absurdity, the sheer contingency of existence, which is its cause. The climax is reached when he decides to return to Paris to write his 'hard as steel' book. Yet we suspect that this is really an anti-climax, for it is hard to see how a book written by a superfluous individual can declare its own inherent necessity and thereby make people 'ashamed of their existence'. The solution to Roquentin's problem does not, we feel, lie here.

On the other hand, we may feel that *La Nausée* is *too* concentrated, that too much of life is omitted and that what Sartre has presented is a distortion. Probably all of us from time to time share the feeling of Roquentin that our own existence is dissolving into Nothingness, but most of us are too busy to attend for long to these private fancies. We have our work to do and our families to support and there are even moments when the banal routines of our day-to-day lives seem to clarify and reveal a glimpse of meaning. It is noteworthy that Sartre himself was aware of the defectiveness of *La Nausée*. In an interview with *Le Monde* in 1964, he said that his novel 'could not act as a counterweight to a dying child'.[7] By this he presumably meant that we cannot afford the luxury of living like Roquentin in a private world when the world outside demands our total attention. Certainly there is nothing in Sartre's novel to counterbalance or alleviate the sense of nausea: all meanings crash down in ruin. Learning, culture, human friendship, even the 'perfect moments' of love – all are destroyed by the rot of absurdity.

Yet as an artist Sartre is surely entitled to concentrate as he does in *La Nausée*, for art may legitimately seek to isolate and define a bit of human experience whose significance is usually lost amid the welter of life. The question we have to ask is whether Sartre succeeds in forcing us to recognize the presence of nausea in ourselves and whether he convinces us that we have paid too little heed to it. Perhaps, like the people of Bouville, we are also guilty of living an unjustified, superfluous existence whose true nature we conceal from ourselves by routine actions and habits of thought. It may be of vital importance that we recognize the implications of nausea and stop thinking of it as a temporary malaise. Salvation may depend upon knowing the worst and shedding delusion.

We may also ask whether Roquentin is more typical of our age than of others, whether his experience is part of what it is like to be 'genuinely human' in the twentieth century. Of course it is easy to think of literary examples of the vanity of life in any period, and the forbears of Roquentin may be found in (for example) Ecclesiastes, Augustine, Shakespeare, and even some forms of Romanticism. Anyone who thinks about the puzzle of human existence must wonder whether life is anything more than a succession of arbitrary events and whether belief in a permanent selfhood or essences of any kind is not simply a delusion. Yet there does seem to be an intensification of this kind of awareness today. Modern literature is full of exiles, outsiders, strangers, rebels – and so also are social studies. We can hardly pick up a serious work without finding ourselves in touch with individuals who feel that they are alienated from any meaningful world, and the vocabulary of alienation has become a recognized essential for any writer who would convince us of his 'realism'. Even James Bond is fundamentally a lonely and rebellious character, though he works for the Establishment, and we suspect that he would not require much brain-washing to make him attempt to murder his employer. There is, indeed, something of a suspicion that alienation has become a cult and that everyone is shouting too loud. We are perhaps enjoying our neuroses.

But there is nothing enjoyable about the nausea of a Roquentin. The fact that a lot of derivative stuff exists should not lead us to think that all nihilism is a pose, and perhaps we need to be warned that the cultivation of nihilistic feelings may be highly dangerous. It is worth remarking that a surprising number of modern writers have committed suicide:* Drieu la Rochelle, Stefan Zweig, Cesare Pavese, Mayakovski, Virginia Woolf, Ernest Hemingway. Others – Malcolm Lowry, Dylan Thomas – drank themselves to death. 'To die voluntarily,' wrote Camus in *The Myth of Sisyphus*, 'implies that one has recognized, at least instinctively, the absurd nature of this habit, the absence of any serious reason for living, the senselessness of this daily agitation and the futility of suffering.' To kill oneself means 'simply to recognize that life is not worth the trouble'.[8] There is a world of difference between a nihilism so terrible and inescapable that it leads to madness or suicide, and a nihilism which is merely a fashionable pose, though it may be doubted whether the latter would exist if the former did not. It is, I think, undeniable that genuine nihilism is more common in the literature of our time than in that of other periods. As Sartre says, we have reached the stage of having to *decide* to live. In an age in which *cosmic* suicide has become possible, such a decision is of literally vital importance.

If we are Christians, we shall not despise the feelings of a Roquentin, nor shall we persuade ouselves that he is merely a poseur. We may think, rather, that nausea is not so far removed from what St Paul called 'the exceeding sinfulness of sin' – the experience of finding that the props of culture, work, social enjoyment, and even religion itself, are shoring up a building

* Silone makes this point in *The Choice of Comrades*.

whose foundations are unsupported. We may, from our point of view, say that nausea is the discovery that our existence is unjustified because we have lost God and cannot create ourselves; that all our substitutes for God are false and useless. We may readily agree with Sartre that man cannot be understood merely in terms of a social or cultural context and that there always comes a point at which we recognize how spurious is the confidence we place in our defensive structures, how easily they crumble away and leave us 'unaccommodated'. But we may also wish to claim that God in Christ is present with us even in the depths of our self-despair.

3

Behind the novels of Sartre stands his Existentialist philosophy, and one wonders whether the characters he invents are more like exemplars of a theory than possible individuals. But Existentialism is not supposed to be a theory about human existence – only one of many rival interpretations – formulated ideologically; it is meant to be descriptive of what it is actually like to be a human being, and that is why it is most appropriately expressed in dramatic form. Even Sartre's major theoretical work, *Being and Nothingness*, is full of homely examples drawn from life.[9] The difficulty is that Sartre, like all morally serious writers, is concerned not only with what men do but also with what they *ought* to do, not only with how they actually understand themselves but with how they *ought* to understand themselves. He wants to break down all the bogus structures, to strip off the layers of falsehood and self-deception, and to reveal the authentic being of man. But this implies a theory about the nature of 'authentic' being which itself stands in need of some authentication. For the most part, Sartre's writings attempt to provide this negatively, by presenting to us a pageant of individuals who are manifestly living *in*authentically and by leaving us to infer from their failure the lines along which we are to look for success. This makes his novels and plays on the whole rather depressing and even inhuman. We are taken into the waste-land but the redeeming passion is not released; we spend a great deal of time on 'bad faith' but very little indeed on 'good faith'; we are inclined to cry, 'The summer is ended and we are not saved.'

Sartre, however, would reply that this is precisely the point at which authentic existence begins – with the feeling of nothingness and absurdity, with the recognition of an unjustified life and acceptance of the challenge to create the self *ex nihilo*. The end of Roquentin's pilgrimage is the discovery that he *can* be free from his own past and from the people in it – including Anny, his former mistress – and can now start his life all over again. Beginning with the absurdity of bare existence from which all dependence on others has been removed, he is now ready to take full responsibility for what he himself can become, for the authentic being which can be generated only from within.

It follows that the sense of meaninglessness by which twentieth-century man is characterized is to his advantage rather than his detriment. In fact, meaninglessness is freedom, the freedom to which we are 'condemned' because we *must* accept final responsibility for ourselves. It is always easier to allow our inner being to be determined by what we are to other people, and to abdicate from the responsibility which demands that all our actions shall be decisively our own; but to be human is to be one for whom existence precedes essence, one whose being is given only through his becoming. Roquentin's nausea is his awareness of unconditioned freedom to create his own essence, to project himself out of the monstrous mass of being, to live at the level of personal, self-determined choice. This is the challenge with which twentieth-century man is faced: to create his own meanings within a meaningless universe, to start from *absolute zero*. The nihilism of our age is in reality its hope.

Sartre has told us that his Existentialism is an attempt to draw out all the implications of a coherent atheistic position.[10] One such implication had already been drawn in *The Brothers Karamazov*: if God does not exist, all is permitted, and in consequence man is abandoned because he finds neither in himself nor outside himself anything he can possibly fasten on to. 'If God existed, the existence of objective values would dispense man from his responsibility of choice. Man would be able to rest himself on the comfortable pillow of ready made certitudes; no longer would he know the anxiety which is the mark of the free man'.[11] Atheism is to be announced as the gospel of man's liberation from all concepts which have the power to define him. Sartre contrasts his own atheism with that of the eighteenth-century philosophers: although they suppressed the idea of God, they still accepted the belief that man is the possessor of a 'human nature', and that each individual is an instance of the universal concept – Man. But if God does not exist, then, says Sartre, 'there is no human nature since there is no God to conceive of it'. Only in the twentieth century, therefore, has the radical freedom of man been plumbed. It is a freedom which starts from nothing: there are no pre-emptions, no paradigms, no models in which the ghost of God may be thought still to linger after his death has been announced. When God goes, all absolutes go with him, and man is left in his individual solitude free at last to become what he decides he will be.

The good news for twentieth-century man is that God does not exist. In his play *Le Diable et le Bon Dieu*, Sartre presents a man called Goetz.[12] He is a German general of late mediaeval times who exults in torture, massacre, treachery, murder. Goetz is proud of the fact that he makes God feel ill at ease, as he says. But someone points out that it is easy to do evil. You can do that without even getting out of bed. The impossible thing is to do good. This is a challenge which Goetz cannot decline. He will prove that he can do good. He will now be on God's side, so he will start his new career with a tremendous advantage and things are bound to turn out well for him. He decides to give all his lands to the poor, but this sparks off a peasants' revolt against the less generous nobility and thousands of the poor are killed. In fact, Goetz causes far more death and suffering in his role as servant of God than he ever did when he was serving the devil. Only one conclusion is possible:

> Heinrich, I am going to let you in on a real bit of mischief. God does not exist. He does not exist. Joy, tears of joy! Alleluia!

Somewhat anachronistically, these words are a parody of Pascal's famous 'Memorial', and no doubt Sartre wants us to see in

Goetz's conversion to atheism the same sense of enlightenment, the same release of energy, as we see in Pascal's experience of God. The trouble with Goetz has been his domination by absolutes: he has tried successively to perform acts of absolute, pure evil, and of absolute, pure good. In both cases he has succeeded only in destroying human lives. But now there are no absolutes – no heaven, no hell, only earth. There is neither God nor devil to blame for men's actions. 'The reign of man,' says Goetz at the end of the play, 'is about to begin . . . I will stand alone with the empty sky above my head . . . There is this war to wage and I will wage it.'

4

The proclamation of atheism as the charter of human freedom reminds us at once of Nietzsche, and his *Thus Spake Zarathustra* is probably a basic document for arriving at an understanding of what is happening in the soul of twentieth-century Western man.

> Before God! But now this God has died! You Higher Man, this God was your greatest danger.
> Only since he has lain in the grave have you again been resurrected. Only now does the great noontide come, only now does the Higher Man become – lord and master!
> God has died: now *we* desire – that the Superman shall live.[13]

This is not so much atheism as what Marcel has called *antitheism*.[14] We are not being told merely that God does not exist, but that God *must* not exist if man is to be born into his great noontide. Perhaps neither Nietzsche nor Sartre offers us a very clear picture of what that noontide will be like, but both are convinced that God has to be eliminated before it will come.

In neither Nietzsche nor Sartre, however, are we supposed to be in the presence of a theoretical, intellectualist nihilism. The death of God is not the conclusion of an argument, leaving us with the danger that some other argument might resurrect him. God has not been argued out of existence – though Sartre does offer arguments: it is more as if God has been murdered, as the Madman tells us in Nietzsche's *Joyful Wisdom*[15] – there is no longer a *desire* that he should exist. So far from our having to make the best of this unfortunate fact and somehow continue to live in spite of it, Nietzsche and Sartre bid us rejoice and enter exultantly into our freedom, welcoming the dawn which has at last broken after the long night of human bondage. The twentieth-century sickness turns out to be convalescence after the illness of faith, and soon we shall rise from our beds and inaugurate the reign of Man, for whom all is now permitted.

In view of the heroism and adventure implied by this gospel, we may be puzzled to know why it is that the writings of Sartre are so depressing. In them, we see people being brought, with tremendous reluctance and struggle, to the starting-line of freedom, but we seldom seem to see them actually running in the promised race. The reason for this is perhaps that it is not really possible for Sartre to make predictions or offer models without denying his own existentialist doctrine. Sartre has repudiated all absolutes and all objective values; man finds himself cast upon a meaningless universe in which there are no sign-posts. no maps, no marked-out routes to follow, not even a concept of human nature from which some sort of guidance may come. Each man must create his own essence and no one else can do it for him. To offer models is to play the part of God and to bring man back into servitude. Sartre will place you at absolute zero, the starting-line of freedom, but after that you are on your own. Absolute zero is a rather depressing spot, which is why Sartre's novels are rather depressing novels.

But Sartre's intense moral seriousness requires him to insist that it is better to be depressed than deluded. To live without God and without ultimate meanings is a difficult calling, and we prefer our delusions, the lies we tell ourselves, because they persuade us that we have a grip on existence. But to be a man in the twentieth century is to see these delusions for what they really are and to be challenged to live without them. We are being summoned by a serious call to a life of responsibility and freedom, to a work of demolition on the spurious orders of belief and convention within which men have been imprisoned throughout the centuries of faith. Like all serious calls, this demands its martyrs and its willing sufferers. Sartre is far from offering us a trivial hedonism or an uncontrolled expression of impulse. The mark of the free man is anxiety because he always feels within himself the nothingness, the senseless absurdity, where his freedom begins, and he knows that, unless he is vigilant, it will claim him utterly. Life, for him, is tragic, for he desires with all his soul to *be* and has to fight unceasingly against non-being, against the terrible forces which threaten to push him over the edge of the abyss. It is small wonder that he finds himself yielding to despair. Roquentin, Goetz, and the other Sartrian heroes are, we feel, unlikely to discover much happiness in their efforts to accept themselves and justify their existence; they are tackling an impossible job. We suspect that Roquentin will wait endlessly for his train to Paris and that it will always be raining over Bouville.

5

Roquentin, I have suggested, has been brought to the starting-line of freedom but we do not see him actually running in the race. In his post-war trilogy of novels entitled *Roads of Freedom*, however, Sartre does attempt to disclose the nature of authentic existence positively instead of by implication. The central character is a professor of philosophy called Mathieu. Up to the point I am about to describe he has been a typically Sartrian figure, aware of the fact that he allows his actions to be dictated by what is outside himself, and never making his own authentic choice. But in the last volume, *Iron in the Soul*, Mathieu has joined the army and we see him as one of a dispirited group of soldiers in defeat. Their unit is scattered, their officers have left them, and their one thought is to surrender easily and quickly to the Germans. Mathieu and a few others, however, decide in the end not to surrender. They station themselves on the tower of a village church, and when the Germans appear they open fire on them.

> He made his way to the parapet and stood there firing. This was revenge on a big scale. Each one of his shots avenged some ancient scruple. One for Lola whom I dared not rob; one for Marcel whom

I ought to have left in the lurch; one for Odette whom I didn't want to kiss. This for the books I never dared to write, this for the journeys I never made, this for everybody in general whom I wanted to hate and tried to understand. He fired, and the Tables of the Law crashed about him – Thou shalt Love thy Neighbour as Thyself – bang! in that bugger's face – Thou shalt not kill – bang! at that scarecrow opposite. He was firing on his fellow men, on Virtue, on the whole world. Liberty is terror. . . . Just time enough to fire at that smart officer, at all the Beauty of the Earth, at the street, at the flowers, at the gardens, at everything he had loved. Beauty dived downwards like some obscene bird. But Mathieu went on firing. He fired. He was cleansed. He was all-powerful. He was free. Fifteen minutes.[16]

If this is meant to be an example of 'authentic' existence, I think it must be admitted that Mathieu's actions are disappointing. There is something childish about a man who pretends to be destroying what he cannot command. Mathieu's action is more like pique than freedom. This is not the kind of behaviour one expects from a professor of philosophy. But perhaps Sartre intends us to react to Mathieu in this way: perhaps he means that Mathieu has disqualified himself from acting resolutely except in this trivial fashion precisely because he *is* a philosopher and has lost himself in a sea of universalism (one assumes that Mathieu is some kind of Hegelian). Certainly, this is the irony of the first novel of the trilogy, *The Age of Reason*.[17] Human existence cannot be rationally ordered or understood, and Mathieu is proof of the fact. So far from enabling him to order his life, philosophy leaves him helpless before the uniqueness of the 'given', which refuses to fit into universal categories. In Mathieu's case, the problem is what to do about the pregnancy of his mistress. When it comes to concrete existence, reason always stumbles over absurdity, and the road to freedom is not the highway of reason but the abyss of the absurd. Mathieu's pilgrimage takes him through the ultimate absurdity of war and defeat, and his final gesture, trivial though it may seem, is for him a magnificent assertion of freedom from his own past. No doubt Sartre has in mind here the exhilarating but suicidal work of the Resistance, and perhaps we are even meant to understand that we are most radically free when, like Mathieu, we choose and create the circumstances of our own death.*

Nevertheless, I do not think we feel *convinced* by this as we read the novel, and in any case it is not the kind of conclusion which seems likely to inspire us to leap forward fearlessly and creatively into the future. The trouble with the novels of Sartre, as has often been said, is their lack of any positive moral content. We have seen that it is hardly possible for Sartre to specify the kind of action which is 'free' and 'authentic' without denying the uniqueness of the challenge to the individual upon which freedom and authenticity depend. The result is that his models are to bizarre and his exhortations too vague to be of much use in helping us as we try to come to grips with the specific reality of our own condition, though we may well agree that 'universal' moral maxims still leave us puzzled before the unique actuality of the moral case and may serve as a refuge from the exigence of individual decision. It is a long time since men discovered that they must not direct their personal lives by unyielding abstract principles. They were told this by someone who had a very poor opinion of men who refused to relieve human suffering on the sabbath day.

6

It is one of the ironies of history that the Christian ethic has been understood in terms which are the opposite of this. The freedom of Jesus to act freely with each fresh situation has been converted into a depressing catalogue of prescribed legislation. As the Grand Inquisitor says, men do not want freedom; they much prefer to have their decisions made for them, and the Church has very readily fallen in with this preference.[18] There is, therefore, a sense in which Sartre and other contemporary writers are recalling us to the kind of life which Jesus himself placed before us – a life, that is, which is creative and open to the future because it is free from stultifying moral prescriptions.

---

* Though it seems that Mathieu was rather improbably meant to survive into a fourth volume in which Sartre intended to 'create a morality'. This volume, however, will certainly not now appear. See the 'Interview' with Sartre in *Encounter*, June 1964.

The difference is that Sartre believes that such a life can be self-generated, whereas Jesus believed it could come only if a man opened himself up to the will of God.

This difference is of course crucial, and it could easily be argued that 'the will of God' brings us back inside the absolutist prison from which Sartre – and other writers – wish to deliver us. How can one be free and creative if one submits oneself to a God who lays everything down in advance? Is not this procedure the very antithesis of freedom, the surrender of all that distinguishes us from the world of objects and entitles us to be called 'human'? Does it not cause men to 'repose on given certitudes' and blind them to the newness of every moment, thus making religion the enemy of the nerve-racking but exhilarating process of *becoming*? Is it not this that has prevented man from entering his great noontide?

The Christian answer to these questions directs our attention to Jesus. He spoke of his own obedience to the Father's will, but we do not get the impression that he was a mere instrument carrying out a programmed operation devised by the Absolute. The New Testament has its equivalents of the Sartrian Nothingness: they are Gethsemane and Calvary, and they represent, not merely a nihilistic *feeling*, but *a deliberate letting go* of all security systems, including even the sense of the divine presence. 'Why hast thou forsaken me?' meant for Jesus that there were no certitudes and that meaning had to be created out of nothing. It was the Father's will to set men free, but this could be done only by the immersion of Jesus in the uncertainty and forsakenness of human life. Freedom had to be actualized through the nihilistic experience itself, because only so could the transcendence of man be established.

The 'transcendence' of man has something in common with Sartre's 'authentic existence' or 'good faith' – indeed, Sartre himself uses the word in the sense that man is 'self-surpassing'. 'Transcendence' means that man cannot be exhaustively described in terms of the physical, social, or other contexts in which his life is lived. In the poetic biblical image, man has eternity in his heart, and he knows himself as one for whom the world provides no correlate which is adequate to his own interior dream. Unamuno has expressed it thus:

> The visible universe becomes all too narrow for me. It is like a cramped cell, against the bars of which my soul beats its wings in vain. Its lack of air stifles me. More, more, and always more! Not to be all and for ever is as if not to be . . .[19]

It is surely this dream of man that causes in him the sense of nothingness and absurdity. At this level of awareness he passes beyond the visible universe and falls into the abyss – or into the eternal. 'The feeling of the vanity of the passing world kindles love in us, the only thing that triumphs over the vain and transitory, the only thing that fills life again and eternalizes it.'[20] When love is kindled, we fall into eternity, into the being of God. When it is not kindled, we fall into the abyss, in company with the heroes of Sartre.

The Christian claim is that the abyss has been spoiled of its terror by Christ, who loved in hell and thereby conquered despair. In him the transcendence of man, that which defines man as the bearer of the divine image, has been recreated. For the freedom of man is not freedom *from* God; it is the freedom *of* God – the freedom in which God began his work of creation out of nothing 'in the beginning'. God's freedom is not the motiveless void of infinite possibility; it is the freedom which has power to express itself in love and to create the response which it desires to find. 'God spoke to the void until it answered back.' The divine freedom was actualized in man by Jesus Christ; in him the human dream became reality when the experience of Nothingness was made the starting-point of God's new creation. The cry of Easter, 'The Lord is risen', marks the end of nihilism and the beginning of freedom. But it is the end of nihilism because the abyss has been plumbed and confronted by Christ.

Roquentin's experience of absurdity is an awareness that existences no longer resonate. Material objects thrust themselves inexplicably towards human consciousness, threatening us by their senseless physicality and forcing us to recognize that they cannot be dissolved into the 'meaning' we have assigned to them. For years we live complacently in the 'order' we have created, unaware of its deceptiveness, until meaning suddenly slides away like a receding tide leaving the world of objects stark and terrifying before us. Objects no longer 'resonate', they do not emit recognizable signals, they do not radiate outwards from themselves and harmonize with other radiations from other objects. And this awareness of inexplicability forces us to experience a like inexplicability *in ourselves*. We also are alienated, we also stand isolated and absurd, like a bean-pole in a desert, unable to find affirmation of our existence in a meaningless world. So we are reduced to absolute zero, to the point at which we experience our existence, not as a reassuring dependence, but as a state of total freedom which is identical with terror and despair.

The greatest Christian thinkers – St Paul, St Augustine, Luther, Pascal – have well understood the kind of annihilating experience which Sartre has described, and they would endorse Sartre's refusal to see in human structures any power to overcome the basic absurdity and terror of existence. The difference is that in Christian thought the nihilation of man has been seen, not in terms of passing subjective moods, but along the permanent perspective of the cross. Despair in the Christian sense is the experience of unaccommodated man when he shares in the forsakenness of the Crucified. For this reason, Christian despair sounds greater depths than the despair of a Nietzsche or a Sartre. As Karl Barth says in his commentary on Romans, the cross passes through 'the whole busy activity of the man of this world'. It does not 'peter out in criticism of this or that concrete thing: it is the final negation of the man of this world and of all his possibilities'.[21] Sartre does not accept that man has been *finally* negated. When all our structures, all our securities have collapsed, one possibility still remains – the 'fundamental project' by which the individual justifies himself against a senseless, threatening world. But the cross negates even this possibility. It goes down into the bottomless abyss where there are no footholds. Man cannot 'project' himself because at this depth of awareness he knows that he has no standing-ground on which to do so. To share in the forsakenness of the Crucified is to accept 'the final negation of man'.

In his book *Theology of Hope*,[22] Moltmann quotes the following striking passage from T. W. Adorno's *Minima Moralia*:

Philosophy, in the only form in which it can still be responsibly upheld in face of despair, would be the attempt to regard all things as they present themselves from the standpoint of redemption. Knowledge has no light save that which shines upon the world from the standpoint of redemption: all else exhausts itself in imitation and remains a piece of technique. Perspectives must be created in which the world looks changed and alien and reveals its cracks and flaws in much the same way as it will one day lie destitute and disfigured in Messiah's light. To attain such perspectives without arbitrariness or force, entirely out of sensitiveness towards things – that alone is the aim of thought.

It is, I think, the achievement of Sartre that he has attained precisely these perspectives in which the world looks changed and alien and reveals its cracks and flaws, though it seems improbable that he would regard himself as a precursor of the Messiah. The point which Moltmann himself is making in this context, however, is that man's 'thinking about the world does not adjust things to the human subject and his imagined needs or his arbitrary prescriptions'. Here, therefore, we must say that the Christian scheme parts company with Sartre, who certainly does not attempt to 'regard things from the standpoint of redemption' but seeks meaning through the projection of the human subject. But such projection, even assuming that it can be made at all, must always leave us with the question whether our individual meanings are not just as deceptive as the public meanings they have supplanted. We need firmer grounds of assurance than this. Christian faith finds them in the resurrection of Jesus Christ and the coming messianic reconciliation which is 'the rectifying future of God'.

For it is as he shares in the forsakenness of the Crucified that man becomes conscious of the divine affirmation. 'The void brought into being by the death of Christ,' says Barth, 'is filled with the new life which is the power of the resurrection.' The resurrection is the affirmation of God which presses into the void and fills it and eternalizes it. We have died with Christ and we know that we shall also live with him. 'Our negative, known, human existence, so little conformed to Jesus, is filled with hope by the positive and secret power of the resurrection.'[23]

Nevertheless, the resurrection triumph does not allow us to

turn Christian faith into another security system and to claim exemption from the forsakenness of Christ. Nietzsche and Sartre are right to repudiate a version of Christianity which suggests that men can abdicate from the terror of freedom and read their lives off from a number of prescribed texts. As Berdyaev says, man loves servitude and easily comes to terms with it. It is *God* who demands that men shall be free, not man himself: 'freedom is not a right of man but a duty of man before God'.[24] I think Camus is not far from the truth when he says that the real passion of the twentieth century is servitude: in our time, the demand for protective structures has led to the inhuman regime of the police state. Nor can it be denied that the Church has been caught up in the obsession for security, and has lived, not in the forward-looking freedom of the Spirit, but in fear lest it lose its tradition. So long as Christianity is understood in these terms it will be the enemy of the creative hazard and the antitheist is right to reject it. But as Moltmann points out, Christian tradition is 'not to be understood as a handing on of something that has to be preserved, but as an event which summons the dead and the godless to life'. The Christian pro-clamation is 'a creative event happening to what is vain, for-saken, lost, godless and dead. It can therefore be designated as a *nova creatio ex nihilo*, whose continuity lies solely in the guaranteed faithfulness of God'.[25] The resurrection faith cannot be dissolved into a static tradition or order or system: it is always a contemporary event, erupting through orders and sys-tems and driving towards the goal of 'the triumph of the resur-rection life over death to the glory of the all-embracing lordship of God'. The Christian task, therefore, is not to call men back from the open horizons of the modern secular hope to a stulti-fying tradition which is supposed to secrete ultimate truth, but rather 'to take these horizons up into the eschatological horizon of the resurrection' where all human hope is transfigured by the reality of God.

For the Christian then, the future lies along the perspective of redemption, which means that the cross and resurrection will constantly be reactualized in human life until the final summing up of all things in Christ. But this does not imply an easy, automatic process by which man is deprived of freedom and responsibility. The resurrection does not cancel out the cross and there is no exemption from the demand of the New Testament that we must die with Christ. The mission of the Church always puts the Church at risk, and the hardest thing for any Church to do is to die to its own past and let itself be reborn into the outward and onward thrust of him who makes all things new. The nihilism of our time cannot be countered by exhortations to project oneself into a void, but still less can it be countered by clinging to a tradition which has lost its explanatory and vitalizing power. 'Anybody who has ever been snatched away from nihilism,' says Helmut Thielicke, 'knows that this does not happen by way of a harmless process of growth and becoming; he knows that he has been laid hold of by a higher hand and drawn across the saving border. We live in the name of this miracle or we vegetate. But we come to this life only if we dare to face the ultimate loneliness of Nothingness. For here all human work ceases; here we come to – the end. But where we come to the end the wonders of God begin.'[26]

Notes

1. 'An Interview with Jean-Paul Sartre' in *Encounter*, June 1964.

2. K. Jaspers, *The Perennial Scope of Philosophy*, Philosophical Library, New York 1949 and Archon Books, 1968, p. 20.

3. J.-P. Sartre, *L'Imagination*, Presses Universitaires, Paris 1936, ch. IV. Eng. trs. by F. Williams, Cresset Press, London 1962.

4. M. Heidegger, *Being and Time*, tr. Macquarrie and Robinson, SCM Press, London 1962, and Harper & Row, New York 1962.

5. J.-P. Sartre, *Nausea*, Hamish Hamilton, London 1962 and Penguin Books, 1965.

6. Anthony Manser, *Sartre, A Philosophic Study*, Athlone Press, London 1966 and Oxford University Press, New York 1966.

7. 'Interview' in *Encounter*, June 1964.

8. A. Camus, *Le Mythe de Sisyphe*, Gallimard, Paris 1942, p. 18. Eng. trs. Hamish Hamilton, London 1955 and Alfred A. Knopf, New York 1955.

9. J.-P. Sartre, *Being and Nothingness*, tr. Hazel E. Barnes, Philosophical Library, New York 1956, and Methuen and Co., London 1957.

10. J.-P. Sartre, *L'Existentialisme est un Humanisme*, tr. in *Existentialism from Dostoevsky to Sartre*, ed. Kaufmann, Meridian Books, Cleveland, Ohio 1956.

11. Charles Moeller, *op. cit.*, Tome II, Casterman, Paris 1957, p. 88.

12. J.-P. Sartre, *Le Diable et le Bon Dieu*, Gallimard, Paris 1951.

13. F. Nietzsche, *Thus Spoke Zarathustra*, tr. R. J. Hollingdale, Penguin Books, Harmondsworth 1961, p. 297.

14. G. Marcel, *The Mystery of Being*, Vol II, The Harvill Press, London 1951, p. 86 and Henry Regnery Co., New York 1951.

15. F. Nietzsche, *The Joyful Wisdom*, tr. Thomas Common, Frederick Ungar Publishing Company, New York 1960, pp. 167-9.

16. J.-P. Sartre, *Iron in the Soul*, Hamish Hamilton, London 1950 and Penguin Books, 1963, p. 225. American title, *Troubled Sleep*, Alfred A. Knopf, New York 1951.

17. J.-P. Sartre, *The Age of Reason*, Hamish Hamilton, London 1947 Penguin Books 1961 and Alfred A. Knopf, New York 1947.

18. F. Dostoevsky, *The Brothers Karamazov*.

19. M. de Unamuno, *The Tragic Sense of Life*, Macmillan, London 1921 and Collins Fontana Books, London 1962, p. 54.

20. Unamuno, *op. cit.*, p. 55.

21. K. Barth, *The Epistle to the Romans*, tr. Hoskyns, Oxford University Press, London and New York 1933, p. 194.

22. Jürgen Moltmann, *Theology of Hope*, SCM Press, London 1967, p. 290f. and Harper & Row, New York 1967.

23. Barth, *op. cit.*, p. 197.

24. N. Berdyaev, *The Divine and the Human*, Geoffrey Bles, London 1949, p. 110 and The Macmillan Co., New York 1949.

25. Moltmann, *op. cit.*, p. 302.

26. H. Thielicke, *Nihilism*, Routledge & Kegan Paul, London 1962, p. 177 and Harper & Row, New York 1961.

3

Phonies and Salauds

Besides the alienated solitaries – the Roquentins – of modern
literature, there are also many examples of their opposites. These
are the persons whom J. D. Salinger calls 'phonies' and Sartre
calls 'salauds'. Other novelists also have their quota of them.
In John Wain's *Hurry On Down*[1] they appear as Robert and
Edith; in Kingsley Amis's *Lucky Jim*[2] the specimen is called
Bertrand Welch; in John Braine's *Room at the Top*[3] his name
is Jack Wales. Although these characters are all different, the
reader begins to think that they must be one person appearing
in different guises, rather as Councillor Lindorf in *The Tales of
Hoffmann* appears as the evil genius in each of the three episodes.
The phony, however, is not an evil man but only a stupid one.
He can usually be recognized by his social success, his insensi-
tiveness, his censorious attitude, and the total lack of any reality
of self behind the public personage. He is, in the opinion of our
authors – or their heroes – very far gone from original righteous-
ness, though he would himself receive this information with
injured incredulity. Let us look at some specimens of him.

Robert and Edith in *Hurry On Down* are the brother-in-law
and sister of the hero's fiancée. We meet them when the hero,
Charles, calls at their house in the hope of seeing his girl. Robert
is a prosperous middle-class tradesman whose disapproval of
Charles, just down from Oxford, is massive and unconcealed. The
author summarizes this disapproval for us by saying that Charles
'did not wear a uniform'. To Robert and Edith, clothes are a
kind of identity-card which immediately and visibly announces
the status of the wearer. But the clothes worn by Charles – non-
committal lounge-suits and heavy shoes – announce no status
and proclaim no identity. Robert is annoyed by Charles' refusal

to fit into a slot, for Robert is the conventionalized Englishman – reliable, no doubt hard-working, a good husband, but a pompous, self-righteous bore. His moustache, Charles notices, is 'curiously non-human . . . as if it had been clipped from the face of an Airedale'. Robert – the human being – has disappeared behind the public personage of the right-thinking, all-too-predictable *bourgeois*. The scene ends when Charles, in a sudden fury of exasperation, throws a bowl of dirty washing-up water over his two critics and leaves the house in a hurry by the back door. He is now, as the title of the novel suggests, on his way down – away from the prison of conventionality inhabited by the Roberts and Ediths, and down into the world of roughs and toughs where it is still possible to be a human being.

Another type of phony is the muscular and philistine football player: to judge from Salinger's *The Catcher in the Rye*,[4] he seems to occupy most of the places in American Universities! One such phony is called Morrow, whose mother, in conversation with the hero of the novel, says that he is very 'sensitive'. The hero is astonished by this evidence of maternal delusion, since to his certain knowledge 'that guy Morrow was about as sensitive as a goddam toilet-seat'. The Morrow type of phony is a young man for whom other people are simply mirrors in which he sees his own reflection; he is quite incapable of entering into their feelings because he never really notices them as people at all. In English novels, the same type is often to be seen in an expensive sports car accompanied by a pretty girl. Such a character is Jack Wales in *Room at the Top*, and he arouses immediate resentment and envy in the breast of the working-class hero, Joe Lampton, who resolves that he 'is going to enjoy all the luxuries which that young man enjoyed'. He will achieve, by brains and cunning, the riches and the social standing which the Jack Waleses of the world have achieved merely by being born into them.

There is a specially unpleasant 'toilet-seat' character in *Lucky Jim*. He is the son of the professor upon whose good opinion the academic future of the hero, Jim Dixon, depends. But we soon realize that Bertrand – the son – is unlikely to help Jim to ingratiate himself with the professor. Bertrand is a bearded artist with a baying voice who immediately arouses in Jim the strongest feelings of antipathy. We know that Bertrand is a phony as soon as we are told about his clothes – 'a lemon-yellow sports coat' with all its buttons fastened – and his beard. Jim feels that the only action he wants from Bertrand is 'an apology, humbly offered, for his personal appearance', and we are not surprised when the two men begin to exchange hostile glances. Bertrand is another of those persons who have to be *seen* in order to *be*, and for whom other people are therefore merely the audience before whom a part is played. If, like Jim, someone in the audience boos instead of applauding, the actor is mightily disturbed. The reason for this is that the part he plays is all there is of the real man – behind the façade there is nothing. The loud appearance conceals a void.

2

The phonies we have looked at so far have been fairly simple souls from whose phoniness most of us may feel reasonably safe. In the case of Morrow, Wales, and Bertrand, the trouble may merely be that they are rather a long time growing up. But the type of person whom Sartre designates a 'salaud' does not allow us to pass this easy verdict. The salaud is like the phony in that he is dependent on other people for his identity, but his dependence is nothing like as obvious or as immature as that of the phony. The difference is that whereas perhaps not many of us are phonies, nearly all of us are salauds.

There is a scene in *Nausea* in which Roquentin is walking round the municipal museum observing the portraits of local worthies which hang on the walls. Each portrait is described and a short biography of its subject is given. Here is a successful man of commerce; here is a noted surgeon; here is a town councillor; here is a mayor and benefactor. And all of them look out upon the world from their portraits with an air of authority. One portrait is described at greater length than the others. It is of a successful business-man who turned to politics and entered the Chamber of Deputies. The theme of his speeches had been the duty of the governing class to govern, to restore the principal of authority; his political writings bore the titles, 'Moral Force', 'The Duty to Punish', 'Will-Power', and 'Labor Improbus'. And there he is in his portrait, sticking his nose impetuously in the air. The joke is that this authoritarian man was only five feet tall! Roquentin remembers this and wants to laugh. 'Of this shrill-voiced little man,' he thinks, 'nothing would go down to posterity except a threatening face, a superb gesture, and the bloodshot eyes of a bull.' The artist had concealed the small stature of his subject.

As Roquentin takes his leave of this gallery of distinguished people, he says, 'Adieu, Salauds'. They are 'salauds' because they are unaware of the nothingness within themselves, the emptiness behind the public façade, behind their assured presentation of themselves to the world. In contrast with the radical honesty of Roquentin's self-awareness, these men think they have a right to exist because of the notice and respect given to them by other people. They are thus examples of what Sartre calls 'bad faith', which means that they have to be seen in order to be.

The process by which the 'salaud' mentality is created is set out in Sartre's story, *The Childhood of a Leader*.[5] This is about a boy called Lucien. He is expected to follow his father as owner and manager of a factory which has belonged to the family for years. The story shows how Lucien gradually assumes the identity of 'leader' and thereby conceals from himself his childhood sense of non-existence. As a boy, he often feels doubtful of his own reality. 'Who am I?' he asks himself, and he answers, 'Now I have it! I was sure of it. *I don't exist*. He closed his eyes and let himself drift. Existence is an illusion because I *know* I don't exist. All I have to do is plug my ears and not think about anything and I'll become nothingness.' Once again, we are, of course, in the presence of *nausea*, only this time it is a *boy's* sense of nothingness, and Sartre perhaps thinks that all children have this kind of doubt about their existence, which is gradually lost as they grow up.* This is what happens in Lucien's case. He finds that he is able to assure himself of his existence

---

* Kipling's Kim and Lewis Carroll's Alice are other examples of children who question their own identity.

by observing the effect he has on other people. Leadership is understood as the power with which a man bears down on his inferiors in order to convince himself that he has an identity. Lucien decides that he *is* someone because he has *rights over others* and he can infer his own reality from their reactions to his authority. The more violent his behaviour, he discovers, the more marked is the response. He gains a particular gratification from sharing in the beating up of a Jew. It is Lucien who lands the final punch, and he then commits himself to membership of a gang of Jew-baiters. He becomes known as 'Lucien who can't stand Jews'. 'The first maxim,' he says to himself, 'is, Not to try to see inside yourself. The real Lucien – he knew now – had to be sought in the eyes of others . . .' His new awareness of himself is summed up in the formula, 'I have rights', and he thinks of the workers at his father's factory waiting for him to exercise those rights. These rights over other people convince him of his right to exist. All he has to do now is grow a moustache. The boy who was conscious of his nothingness has become a 'salaud'. He has discovered the trick of looking for his own existence in other people.

3

In the case of Lucien, the means by which he assures himself of his existence are violence and authoritarianism. The 'salaud' technique can, of course, take many forms, though its purpose is always the same – to get oneself noticed and known so that other people will reflect back the identity one has assumed.* The salaud is to himself precisely what he is to the public, and he therefore needs the public in order to grasp his own existence.

Sartre excels at showing how much our inner life, what we are to ourselves, is built up by the identity we appear to have under the gaze of others. We all find ourselves playing a part, assuming a role, until our freedom to create ourselves is lost and we simply become the part we are playing. The waiter in the

* This is a frequent theme in Sartre's writings. The 'salaud' category embraces such diverse characters as a pretty girl walking along the street (*Intimacy*) and a homicidal paranoiac (*Erostratus*).

café is a little *too* attentive to the customers: he handles the dishes with a little too much flourish and expertise.* Why? Because he is *playing* at being a waiter, he is assuming a role at which others can look.[6] So it is that our inner emptiness can be concealed by the conventionality of the role we have assumed. The way of freedom, of authentic existence, demands that we fight against this gaze of others, which, like that of Medusa, turns us into stone and makes us our own statues where we are fixed in a meaning which is false because it is imposed on us by 'others'.

To be fixed for ever in a role which we *recognize* to be false – that is Hell, and its power is not the devil's but other people's. This is the theme of Sartre's play, *Huis Clos*,[7] which contains the notorious line, 'There is no need for the rack. Hell is other people.' Three people are pictured in Hell, which is depicted, not inappropriately, as a bedroom in a provincial hotel furnished in the style of the second empire. Each of these people – two women and a man – has died in shameful circumstances, and each wants to change his or her identity for a better one. For this, they need each other – in fact they are now eternally dependent on each other in order to exist at all. Garcin, the man, has died a coward and has therefore left behind him in the world an image of himself as a coward. So his only hope now is to get the two women who are in hell with him to deny his cowardice and to think of him as a hero. One of the women falls in love with him, and the other (Estelle) points out that the former's opinion of Garcin is worthless, because 'a woman will tell a man he is God the Father' if it will help her to get him. So Garcin turns to her and asks, 'Estelle, am I a coward?' But Estelle refuses to play the game as he wants it played. 'You must decide that for yourself', she replies, and this, of course, is precisely what Garcin cannot do. Only if *other people* deny his cowardice can he convince himself of his heroism. So he is a coward for ever because there is no one willing to tell him otherwise. Hell is other people.

But above all it is the gaze of *God* that petrifies us and fixes

---

* He is, presumably, a French waiter. For a very different kind of waiter (English) see *Lucky Jim*.

us in a false role. Before him we are sinners and have no power
to create ourselves. In his novel *The Reprieve*,[8] Sartre presents
a great variety of people all of whom are grasping at any means
by which they can evade the necessity of making resolute decisions. The period of the novel is just before the second world
war when the western democracies were living in the deluded
state of 'appeasement', afraid to come to grips with evil. From
Chamberlain and Daladier down to a crude character called
'Gros Louis', everyone in Sartre's work is looking for a reprieve.
One young man named Daniel blames his cowardice on God
and gives up the hopeless struggle to be different. 'Here am I,'
he says to God, 'as thou hast made me, a vile coward, irredeem-
able. Thou lookest at me and all hope departs. I am weary of my
efforts to escape myself. I shall enter (a church), I shall stand
among those kneeling women like a monument of iniquity. I
shall say, I *am* Cain. Well, thou hast made me, now sustain me.'
Daniel believes that he bears the indelible mark of Cain, the
mark made by God which fixes him for ever in a shameful
identity. Cain was a murderer, Daniel is only a coward, but each
of them is bound to play his divinely appointed role to the end.
There is no appeal against the divine verdict. God is other
people absolutized. 'Religion' is thus acceptance of oneself as a
salaud and surrender of the responsibility to be *for-oneself*. It is
better to be Cain than to be nothing. To stand under the accusing gaze of a baleful deity is to be assured of existence and to
be saved from non-being. Daniel's 'conversion' is simply a way
of evading the terrible freedom to create his own essence. He
has accepted the identity of Cain because the alternative is to
have no identity at all.

4

There is, it must be conceded, a certain kind of morbid religi-
osity which enjoys cultivating feelings of guilt, and Sartre may
be right in thinking that this is the only way by which some
people can grasp their existence. One is reminded of the remark
of Clamence in Camus's novel *The Fall*, that there are those who
climb on to the cross only in order that they may be seen from

a greater distance. Berdyaev thought that the Church itself had
been 'overwhelmed by the depressing consciousness of sin' and
had therefore failed to maintain the creative freedom of the
Spirit.[9] But it is the heart of the New Testament message that
God does not allow us to become fixed for ever in our state of
guilt and failure. Even the Old Testament prophets, with their
almost obsessional sense of divine judgment, do not think of
condemnation as God's final word; if men are able to hear the
word of condemnation, they may then be able to hear the word
of blessing. 'I, even I, am he that blotteth out thy transgressions
for my own sake; and I will not remember thy sins.'[10] God's
remembrance of man is in the pain which he shares with him:
he has engraved man on the palms of his hands; he has pleaded
with him, agonized with him, fought for him. These vivid biblical images do not describe a God who fixes man in his guilt.
They describe a God who judges in order to liberate, who accepts
men as they are, in the falsity of their sin, in order that they may
become other than they are, in order that they may share the
divine freedom and become 'authentically' themselves. To quote
Berdyaev again,[11] the relations between God and man are not
forensic but dramatic, and it is above all in Jesus Christ that we
discover the *dynamic* nature of the divine-human encounter.
It was precisely in order that men might be *freed* from the
petrifying effect of guilt and self-rejection that Christ died on the
cross: our charter of liberty is not the death of the theistic God
but *the death and resurrection of the God-man*. In Jesus we learn
that God is not a mere spectator of the human scene, but a
participant in it, and that his will for man is not condemnation
but re-creation. Even the mark of Cain in the Genesis story is
probably to be understood not as a sign that he is a murderer
but as a sign that he is under divine protection. What is suggested
here is not the endlessness of divine condemnation, but the limitless range of the divine will to save.

Nevertheless, we must admit the force of Sartre's analysis of
the 'salaud' mentality and agree that what we are to ourselves is
at least partly determined by the role we play in relationship to
other people – especially, perhaps, if that role is a 'professional'
one. Surprisingly often, a man 'looks like' what he is. Many

parsons actually *are* like 'stage' parsons, many Oxford dons seem to carry their senior common room about with them, many pig-keepers resemble their charges, and so forth. No doubt Sartre has done well to call our attention to the danger we are in of disappearing behind our façades and becoming wholly identified with the part we play. The word 'salaud', spoken to oneself when professional *hubris* is strong, may have a usefully deflating effect comparable to that of Mad Margaret's 'Basingstoke'.[12]

But it is surely rather excessive to think that *all* our human relationships have a falsifying effect upon our own individuality. To seek to abstract ourselves from the social context in order to create our central being in isolation, and to act always in the light of a detached interior conviction, is a highly artificial procedure by which we are more likely to end up in the state of Peer Gynt's onion – without any centre at all. It would also, one would think, be rather bad for the nervous system. We may well feel that we should remove ourselves from as much social triviality as possible and decline to share in many of the conventional forms of time-wasting, though even these may have unexpected rewards. But most of us certainly have reason to be grateful to our relatives and friends and to those who have their places in the wider context of our lives. One suspects that one would be less, not more, of a man without them, in spite of the exasperation they sometimes cause in us.

The curious mixture of attraction and repulsion which we find in our relations with others is well caught by Arthur Koestler in his autobiography, *The Invisible Writing*:

> At times I feel literally stifled and choked by loneliness. For instance, I am sitting alone in my room, reading a book. The others are playing in the garden . . . Suddenly I stop reading . . . The whole room trembles with loneliness . . . Then I want to join the others . . . But I have hardly been two minutes with them and it is all gone. They bore me. They are primitive. I can't talk to them . . . I feel even lonelier in the garden than I did in my room. I hurry back to my room, and the whole thing starts afresh.[13]

Koestler is here writing of childhood, in which this kind of experience is more common than in adult life; but perhaps we never lose the feeling that the claims of autonomous selfhood and our need of the society of other people, both of which are equally imperious, are contradictory. Yet it is a mistake to try to live on only one side of the contradiction. Extreme individualism is no more 'authentic' than acceptance of oneself as a 'salaud'. Human reality exists across the two poles of separateness and participation, and it becomes impossible to be 'genuinely human' when the polarity is destroyed.

This leads us to question the absence of a whole dimension of human experience from the Sartrian estimate, and that is – *participation*. One is struck by the extreme individualism of Sartre. Authentic being seems to involve a repudiation of all sharing in the being of another. There is no *love* in Sartre's work : relations between the sexes are always portrayed in terms of the demands imposed by one partner upon the other, so that love becomes an irksome infringement of liberty. Even the *emotion* of love is considered by Sartre to be entirely possessive,[14] and is never seen as a participation in the feelings of another person in which the individual finds enrichment through self-giving. Sartre seems to think that the self must always be projected *against* the Other because the Other is always a threat to one's subjectivity. This view is, of course, backed up by his distinction between the 'in-itself' and the 'for-itself', between static being which has no power to define itself, on the one hand, and the dynamic freedom of 'existence' on the other.[15] A stone has 'being', but only man has 'existence' because only he has power to define and create his own essence. The danger of love is that it allows the Other to treat us as an 'object', which means that we become what the Other decides we shall be and lose the power to define ourselves.

Sartre's view may well be correct at the two extremes of uncommitted sex and self-negating infatuation, but it is surely a bizarre description of what we usually understand by 'love'. What Sartre seems to miss is the experience of being grasped by the Other in a way which seems to enrich our *self*-awareness and by which we are liberated from our involuted subjectivity. Separateness and participation are always in tension, but they are not mutually exclusive choices.

So they lov'd, as love in twain
Had the essence but in one;
Two distincts, division none:
Number there in love was slain.[16]

The problems raised by separateness and participation also occur in the relationship of the individual to the wider human context of the society. Our inability to communicate with others, the erosion of personal liberty, and the widespread estimate of the individual in terms of his 'function' and his 'statistical profile', are all supposed to be twentieth-century diseases. Marcel has said that our society has become fragmented and atomized, so that we all exist in a state of alienation and are in danger of becoming merely what our dossiers say we are: a name, an address, an occupation, and so on. In these conditions, our inner life, what we are to ourselves, dries up, and we can no longer communicate as human beings because we no longer have within us the means for doing so.[17] But Marcel does not shut us up, as Sartre seems to do, in the two alternatives of insincerity and emptiness. Our relationship with tradition, convention, and organization need not be a fall into mere functionalism. As Raymond Williams says, 'All depends upon the depth of our own individual commitment and the clarity of our individual purpose', and he goes on to point out that the individual who sees himself as a *member* of the society to which he belongs will accept its values as his values, its purposes as his purposes, 'to such an extent that he is proud to describe himself in its terms'.[18] So far from feeling that the society is opposed to him, 'he looks upon it as the natural means by which his own purposes will be forwarded'. Even in a revolutionary situation the individual is still bound to the society. 'The real crisis of authentic and inauthentic is both an individual and a social process . . . the stages of growth which constitute the integration of a man as a personal individual will inevitably be forms of relationship with the whole organization of his society.'[19] Again we find that separateness and participation are not mutually exclusive. The ideal society is one in which selfhood and cohesion are both maximum, and this does not exclude the possibility that the action of the individual in the society and his commitment to its service may have about them a quality of protest *against* the society, even while he draws much of his own strength from those among whom he labours and from the love of his friends. 'Deprived of society,' says Lewis Mumford, 'the ego loses any confining sense of its own proper dimensions: it swings between insignificance and infinity, between self-annihilation and world-conquest; between the hidden Sorrows of Werther and the visible triumphs of Napoleon; between the desperation of suicide and the arrogance of godhead.'[20]

5

When we seek to extend this human context, with its tension between the individual and the society, into the divine context, we find ourselves thinking of the doctrine of the Trinity. Here we learn that the paradox of human nature is the same as the paradox of the divine nature: the divine life is itself a participation of persons in a unity of existence. In God, both the separateness and the participation are at their ideal limits. God separates himself from himself in the Son, yet both participate in the unity of the Spirit. We must say that it is not man as an isolated individual but man-in-community who reflects the divine image: to be human is to have the power of participating in the subjectivity of others, and the source of this power is in the divine being. The curse of Babel is a symbolization of the fact that man's power of participation has been greatly weakened because he has repudiated his dependence on God and has thereby become isolated from his fellow men. That is why Christ's work of reconciliation included the creation of a participating community, made possible by the unifying power of the Holy Spirit which, on the day of Pentecost, overcame the curse of Babel. Jesus told the disciples that they were in him as he was in the Father:[21] the oneness of the Church was to be the actualization in the world of the divine community, manifested in mutual acceptance and creative love. The Church is meant to be nothing less than a reflection of the Trinitarian God, though we have to admit that it is a faint reflection and will no doubt remain so until the summing up of all things in Christ.

In the traditional statement of Trinitarian doctrine which we call the Athanasian Creed, we are warned against 'confounding the Persons' of the Godhead on the one hand, and 'dividing the Substance' on the other. If it is true that man-in-community is meant to be a kind of counterpart to God-in-community, then we should expect that heresies about the Trinity would also be heresies about Man. This, I believe, is exactly the case. If we 'confound the persons' in the human sense, we become upholders of collectivism, fascism, political absolutism of all kinds – the view that the individual has no personal identity or significance apart from his membership of the State or Party. Confounding the persons in the human context means failing to recognize the status of the unrepeatable individual, the unique human person who has a right to be an end in himself. To 'divide the substance', on the other hand, is to create or condone apartheid, racialism, class privilege, inequality of wealth and opportunity. For here we are denying the fact of our common humanity, our mutuality as human beings dependent upon one another for our well-being and fullness of life, our obligation to all who have the gift of manhood or womanhood, our grounding with them in the basic reality of our human nature. It is not hard to see that both these heresies are highly characteristic of our century.

If the Christian claim is right – namely, that Christ has brought us into the community of the divine life and that the Spirit has created the Church to be the counterpart of that life in the world – then we should expect to find in the Church a unique combination of individual freedom and participating community. We should expect redemptive power to show itself in care and respect for the individual together with a thrust across all the boundaries by which men are divided from one another. The Church is not a collective in which the individual has to let himself be defined by some standardized profile which turns him into a 'salaud'; but neither is it a dispersion of windowless monads having no share in community of being. Christ brings under question both the self-assertion *and* the self-negation of man, both isolationism and collectivism. What we discover is that man finds his full individual self only when he belongs to a community in which there is the power of participation. The richness of this fellowship is increased by the individual gifts of its members: the richness of the individual is increased by his mutuality with others in a shared communion of being. Christ is not divided by differences of emphasis in doctrine or ecclesiastical organization or custom. But he *is* divided by the reassertion in Christians of the curse of Babel.

As Tillich has said, the distinctiveness of the Church's unity lies in its power to take into itself more and more diversity. Unity without diversity is simply a kind of death, and if unity were to mean the evening out of differences, then there could be no more participation. The power of participation is potentially greatest when the diversity of the participants is greatest, for participation is not the absorption of one being by another but a dynamic relationship of giving and receiving. This means that the Church loses its true definition when it becomes a closed, self-perpetuating society of like-minded people. It must ever seek to draw into itself and to be enriched by the diversity of men and women, of races and nations. Or, to put it another way, the Church must strive to empty itself into the world. The Church cannot be more than a very imperfect reflection of the divine unity until it embraces all mankind. And if we feel that this scale of millions is too gigantic to be comprehensible, and that our own part in so vast a company is negligible, we may remind ourselves that there is no limit to God's knowledge of his creatures and no limit to the power of participation we can have in him.

> God gave all men all earth to love;
> But, since our hearts are small,
> Ordained for each one spot should prove
> Belovèd over all.[22]

In Christ we still have the 'one spot', but we know it to be part of the far greater whole in which it adds its own contribution in the totality of being.

6

In her excellent book on Sartre, Iris Murdoch says: 'We know that the real lesson to be taught is that the human person is precious and unique; but we seem unable to set it forth except in terms of ideology and abstraction.'[23] Her point is that Sartre, for all his existentialist claims, is really trying to construct a big theoretical machine and somehow gear it on to the practicalities of life. The Christian belief is that only a *person* could set before us the complexities, the ambiguities, and the creative possibilities of man: a person who had no easy prescription to offer, but whose own life was rich in freedom and creativeness, who came to minister and to give his life for many. To those who have seen Christ in this way, the writings of Sartre seem to cry out for the Gospel: much of his work appears to depict the very condition of man which the Bible indicates by such terms as sin, slavery, hardness of heart, unrighteousness, wrath, and the rest. Indeed, some of the words Sartre himself uses in his analysis of man are borrowed from the Christian vocabulary, and his special brilliance lies in his ruthless display of human distortion and of the 'unjustified' state of twentieth-century man. In Sartre, everything seems to go bad on us – even what is highest and best in man becomes deformed and trivialized. The exceeding sinfulness of sin has seldom been more relentlessly exposed by one writer. It is hard to see what is left for us except the leap of faith, and hard to understand why Sartre does not make it – unless, as is probable, his doctrine of social and political *commitment*, which it is not easy to reconcile with his immoderate individualism, represents such a leap. Sartre considers his philosophy to be a philosophy of *action*, and there is an implied contrast here with Christianity which he thinks is characterized by complacency and inertia. It is not enough merely to say that Sartre misconceives the nature of Christianity: we ought to ask what is wrong with our witness to it that a man of Sartre's intransigent honesty and hard-headedness, an extreme but by no means untypical figure of our age, is prevented from seeing its realism and its promise. On the other hand, have *we* ever understood the full depth of human need which Sartre has entered and set before us, or has our faith become the kind of sheltering structure which Sartre rightly wishes to tear down? No doubt there is far more of the 'salaud' about us than we realize.

Notes

1. John Wain, *Hurry On Down*, Secker and Warburg, London 1953 and Penguin Books, 1960. American title *Born in Captivity*, Alfred A. Knopf, New York 1954.

2. Kingsley Amis, *Lucky Jim*, Victor Gollancz, London 1954, Penguin Books, 1961 and Doubleday & Co., Garden City 1954.

3. John Braine, *Room at the Top*, Eyre and Spottiswoode, London 1957, Penguin Books and Houghton Mifflin, Boston 1957.

4. J. D. Salinger, *The Catcher in the Rye*, Hamish Hamilton, London 1951, Penguin Books, 1958 and Little, Brown & Co., Boston 1951.

5. J.-P. Sartre, *Intimacy*, Neville Spearman, London 1949, Panther Books, 1966 and New Directions, Conn. 1952.

6. *Being and Nothingness*, p. 59.

7. J.-P. Sartre, *Théâtre*, Gallimard, Paris 1947.

8. J.-P. Sartre, *The Reprieve*, Hamish Hamilton, London 1947, Penguin Books, 1963 and Alfred A. Knopf, New York 1947.

9. N. Berdyaev, *Esprit et Réalité*, Aubier, Paris 1943.

10. Isaiah 43.25 (RV).

11. N. Berdyaev, *The Divine and the Human*, p. 111.

12. Gilbert and Sullivan, *Ruddigore*, Act 2.

13. A. Koestler, *The Invisible Writing*, Hamilton and Collins, London 1954, pp. 236-7 and Beacon Press, New York 1955.

14. J.-P. Sartre, *The Emotions*, tr. B. Fretchman, Philosophical Library, New York 1948.

15. *Being and Nothingness*.

16. Shakespeare, *The Phoenix and the Turtle*.

17. G. Marcel, *The Mystery of Being, Vol. I*, Harvill Press, London 1950, ch. 2.

18. R. Williams, *The Long Revolution*, Chatto and Windus, London 1961, Penguin Books, 1965, p. 102 and Columbia University Press, 1961.

19. Williams, *op. cit.*, p. 104.

20. L. Mumford, *The Condition of Man*, Secker and Warburg, London 1944, Mercury Books, 1963, p. 290 and Harcourt, Brace & World, New York 1944.

21. John 14.20.

22. R. Kipling, *Sussex*, Macmillan.

23. I. Murdoch, *Sartre*, Bowes and Bowes, Cambridge 1953, p. 76 and Yale University Press, 1953.

4

Ghosts and the King

I have suggested that it is possible to criticize Sartre's estimate of man for its failure to recognize the part played by *participation* in the development of the individual. Sartre suggests that human relationships are essentially relationships of *conflict*, because the Other is always felt as a threat to selfhood which necessitates the projection of the self *against* the Other. It would be foolish to deny that this often seems to be true, but I have argued that it arises because of the polarity of separateness and participation in human relations – a polarity which can be wrongly felt to be a *contradiction*. Sartre is right to warn us against the danger of as it were failing to maintain the pole of separateness, but he is wrong in thinking that this can be done only by refusing participation. If Sartre were objecting, not to participation but to something like functionalism or collectivism, we should readily agree with him. It must be admitted that there are good reasons for Sartre's insistence on the choice of the self in a world in which the individual is more and more vulnerable to the kind of falsification which Sartre has described so well.

Perhaps the most striking instance of this falsification is to be seen in the White estimate of the Negro, which is exactly what Sartre means by that gaze of the Other which imposes a false identity. The most impressive endorsement of his analysis of the human condition has been its profound effect on African writers and artists since about 1946. For them, the demand to choose oneself, to repudiate definition by the Other, to live authentically, has undoubtedly been a powerful inspiration. The effect is seen in the movement known as 'Présence Africaine' which started among French-speaking Africans in the late 1940s. Its leaders were Léopold Sédar Senghor of Senegal, Aimé Césaire

of Martinique, and Léon Damas of French Guinea. It may have
been Aimé Césaire who invented the term 'Négritude' to signal-
ize the inspiration of the movement. By it was meant a deliberate
exploration of what it meant to be black and a newly-found
pride in all that differentiates the black peoples from the white.

Sartre's own views about what it is like to be a Negro are
worth quoting. 'The Negro cannot deny that he is a Negro,
nor claim for himself this abstract colourless humanity (that is,
of being merely "a man among men"); he is black.' But this
'facticity' – by which Sartre means a givenness which is nevertheless *not* determinative of personal reality and need not obstruct
the fundamental 'project' of the self – of the Negro's colour is
a threat to his choice of himself only if he acquiesces in the white
estimate of it as a mark of inferiority and servitude. The point
is, however, that the Negro need not accept this estimate: he
can, as it were, *choose* to be a Negro; he can be proud of his
colour, and the very struggle demanded by the white estimate
will compel him to live 'authentically'. It is part of Sartre's
general thesis that we recognize our freedom in our recognition
of the facts of our condition which deny it; we cannot be aware
of freedom without being aware of that which opposes freedom.*
The Negro cannot be other than black: it is part of his 'facticity'. But he can, for that very reason, respond the more intensely
to the demand of freedom and can choose to be himself *against*
the white man's estimate. 'He is compelled to be authentic,'
says Sartre; 'insulted, enslaved, he stands up, he picks up the
word "Negro" that has been thrown at him like a stone, in the
face of the white man he claims with pride to be black.'

That quotation is from an article in which Sartre introduced
an anthology of African poetry which appeared in 1948,[1] the
very year in which Césaire's poem *Cahier d'un retour au pays
natal*, a foundation work of Négritude, was published. The connection is surely not accidental. It can hardly be doubted that
the African exponents of Négritude, most of whom were edu-

* This may be illustrated by Sartre's paradoxical statement, 'We have
never been more free than under the German occupation' (*Situations III*,
Gallimard, Paris 1949, p. 11). Man is rather like a loudspeaker, which
operates more efficiently if it is made to work against a load of air.

cated in Paris and some of whom settled there for a time, were influenced by Sartre. One therefore feels some surprise that Anthony Manser should refer to the passage I have quoted as 'romantic nonsense'. As I hope to show, Négritude has serious limitations; but I do not think that an estimate which played a not inconsiderable part in producing it can be described as 'nonsense', though it may certainly deserve the epithet 'romantic'.

2

It should be said at once that there is a great difference between the attitude of Negro writers who work within a dominating Western culture and that of African writers who work within continental Africa itself. On the whole, Négritude has been a product of the former rather than the latter, though of course the movement has not been lacking in African adherents, especially in those countries where European culture has penetrated deeply. But it would be a mistake to think that all continental African writers are as committed to the search for an African identity as are those who live in the European and American dispersion. With the tragic exception of the white-dominated African territories, the African writer today has little reason to feel threatened by the white world, though this is not to say that he has not felt threatened in the past. Certainly there is pride in African tradition and achievement, but it is not the neurotic pride of those who find themselves compelled to fight for their identity in an alien land. Negro writers who try to reach back through the generations to a definitive Africanism are probably deluding themselves. When a foreign Negro visits the African continent he very quickly discovers that common colour is by no means the same thing as common identity, and he has to face the deep forsakenness of being a stranger in the very place where he had expected to feel fully at home. There is no sign that the gap is getting less, and it seems unlikely that the doctrine of universal Négritude will ever emerge from the realm of ideology into that of fact.

In spite of doubts about the possibility of Négritude as a viable doctrine in the modern world, however, we should make no mistake that we have witnessed in Africa what Max Warren calls 'a profound revolution of the human spirit',[2] a deliberate choice of the self which must precede and is indeed a precondition of revolution in political and social action. I believe that African writing, in its purposeful celebration of Africanness, gives to Sartrianism a reality and depth which, for all his existentialist claims, Sartre's own writings have never really achieved. Négritude does exhibit the strength of the fundamental project by which selfhood is posited. The freedom which the African has claimed is not merely freedom from imperial rule: it is the choice which orders all other choices – the decision to live in the light of one's own interior conviction and to be committed to it as to an absolute.

As I have suggested, the *ideology* of Négritude has come mostly from those who live or have lived outside the independent nations of black Africa itself, and we find among them a strong conviction of African uniqueness and a determination to create an 'African' personality against the European estimate. For some, this determination has included a total rejection of European political systems and cultural influences. Here is a very 'Sartrian' expression of Négritude by one of its leading exponents, Aimé Césaire. He is writing an open letter to Maurice Thorez who was then (1956) secretary of the French Communist Party, in which he explains his reasons for resigning from the Party. It is, one may remark, rather ironical to find an African writer repudiating on what are virtually Sartrian grounds the very Party with which Sartre himself has been associated.* Césaire writes:

A fact of capital importance in my eyes is this: we men of colour, at this precise moment of historical evolution, have, in our consciousness, taken possession of the entire field of our singularity, and we are ready to assume, for every plan and throughout every domain, the responsibilities which flow from this awareness. The singularity of our 'situation in the world' which is not to be confounded with any other; the singularity of our problems

* Though Sartre himself pointed out in 1948 that the Negro could not count on the help of the *prolétariat blanc* – because 'it profits from colonization'. *Situations III*, p. 237.

which belongs to no other problem; the singularity of our history, cut up by terrible avatars which belong only to itself; the singularity of our culture, which we want to see become more and more a living reality.

Césaire condemns the French CP for

their conviction of the omnilateral superiority of the West; their belief that the kind of evolution which has operated in Europe is the only kind of evolution; that it is by way of this evolution that the entire world must pass.

And he goes on,

For my part, I believe that the black people are rich in energy and passion; that they lack neither vigour nor imagination; but that these forces can only wither away in organizations which are not their own, made by themselves and adapted to ends which they alone are able to determine . . . We want our society to raise itself to a higher degree of development, but by itself, by inward conviction, by interior necessity, without anything from outside coming in to undermine that conviction, or to alter it or to compromise it.[3]

One salutes Césaire's letter as a noble utterance, yet without quite being able to suppress doubts about its realism. One feels like remarking that Césaire could hardly have said this at all without his highly literate use of the French language, and that his repudiation of European culture is therefore compromised in the very process of stating it. However much he may wish to assert the 'singularity' of Africa, the African writer is up against the fact that he cannot easily do so except in terms which are themselves products of European thought.

So far as actual language is concerned, this difficulty is sometimes far less apparent in the creative writing of continental Africa, where the English language particularly may be used in African idioms which are fresh and even startling. The Nigerian novelist Amos Tutuola is well known for his use of 'West African English' in his novels, which has some right to be classified as a different language from 'English English' and certainly conveys a powerful impression of genuine Africanness.

I think it can fairly be claimed that Césaire's letter witnesses to the strength of the Sartrian estimate; but it also witnesses to its weakness, its imbalance. What we are now beginning to see is that Négritude is a temporary, if necessary, phase in the evolution of Africa. Already much of the early force of the movement seems to be spent, and the palm is passing from French-speaking to English-speaking African writers. It is well known that in the old colonial days the British Government did not adopt the policy of cultural assimilation practised by the French, and this may partly account for the fact that in the African writing which is coming from the former British territories – Nigeria, Ghana, and Sierra Leone in the West, and Kenya, Uganda, Tanzania and Zambia in the East – there is very little self-conscious Négritude. Some writers, indeed, would repudiate it altogether. Wole Soyinka of Nigeria has asked whether it is necessary for a Tiger to proclaim its Tigritude, though one might well feel like replying that that is precisely what a tiger *does* do! Nevertheless, it is clear that Négritude is now seen to be insufficient as an artistic motive: there are other areas to occupy, more universal themes to explore.

The move beyond Négritude, however, was already being made in 1956. At the Congrès des Ecrivains et Artistes Noirs held in Paris in that year,[4] the question was raised whether it might not be the African task to *reconcile* the cultures of black and white and go beyond them both. Amos Tutuola's novel *The Palm Wine Drinkard* was cited at the Congress as a book by an African writer which spoke with equal truth to the experience of both black and white, and James Baldwin, in his report on the Congress, comments on this that perhaps 'part of the great wealth of the Negro experience lay precisely in this double-edgedness'. The speaker, says Baldwin, 'was suggesting that all negroes were held in a state of supreme tension between the difficult, dangerous relationship in which they stood to the white world, and the relationship, not a whit less painful or dangerous, in which they stood to each other. He was suggesting that in the acceptance of this duality lay their strength.'

What this speaker at the Congress seems to have been contesting was the view that the African writer must operate only inside his own artistic ghetto, with its assumption that he can ignore the deep penetration of his own culture by that of Europe which is already an indisputable fact. The aim must rather be to create an African art out of the very conflict of black with white and thereby contribute, not to a restricted 'African' vision of man, but to a *total* vision. Négritude would then become the African way of understanding the puzzles of human life which, with differences of emphasis and detail, are common to all men. The mistake of Césaire, we may suggest, was the Sartrian mistake of supposing that the individual could be 'authentic' only if he refused the influence of the Other. This refusal might well be a necessary initial protest by the African against devaluation, but it should not continue to be the sole definition of his artistic intention. When we read African writing, we should find ourselves compelled to say, not merely 'So this is what the African is like', but also 'So this is what *I* am like'.

It is all too easy to fall into the error of supposing that continental African writing is homogeneous: in fact, of course, it is highly diverse. Bantu writing from South Africa is filled with the anguish of apartheid, and, as Ezekiel Mphahlele has said, Négritude is merely so much intellectual talk to those who have to come to terms with a multi-racial society. As one would expect in view of the fact that there are no white settlers there, West African writers are not nearly so conscious of the bitterness of this struggle. There is great variety among Nigerian novelists, from the sophisticated 'Westernism' of an Achebe or an Aluko, to the mythological 'Africanism' of a Tutuola. There are differences in content and attitude as well as style. Some writers are concerned to go behind Western influence and to recapture the rhythms and values of the 'old' Africa; others direct themselves to an exploration of the conflict between old and new, and pose radical questions about the disruptive effects of social and cultural change; others again treat the old Africa dismissively, and welcome not only material betterment but also the secularism and individualism which accompany it.

3

As an example of a book which is African in its expression and detail but approaches the universal in its human disclosure, let

us take Tutuola's novel *My Life in the Bush of Ghosts*.[5] This is
a story based on the African belief that the Bush or Wilderness
is inhabited by spirits which have a malign envy of the living
and represent the chaos of existence when it is unsupported by
the order and values of human community. A boy aged seven is
driven by tribal war into the Bush, and the story tells of his
encounter with the forces of disorder and of his eventual return
home having survived their grisly horrors. The ghosts in the
Bush are hideous and some of them stink: they remind us of
the soft, monstrous masses of disorder which were at the heart
of Roquentin's 'nausea'. Tutuola's ghosts are mere existences,
separated from the meaningful order which the living enjoy and
incapable of reasoned action. The boy in the story summarizes
his adventures in the words, 'This is what hatred did' – by which
he means the hatred of a polygamous household which failed
to protect him during his mother's absence. Tutuola seems to
be asserting the preciousness of communal values and the senselessness of an existence which is deprived of them. The Bush
appears as an exaggerated form of the disorder which the boy
had known in his own family and village. It is disorder that is
the main feature of the Bush – irrationality rather than demon-
ism. 'Ghosts have no arrangements for anything at the right
time and the right place.' Form and substance are separable:
the human shape can be changed at will into that of an animal,
and purpose is constantly frustrated by absurd interventions. For
Sartre, the experience of disorder, the absence of essences, is
the point at which human freedom begins as the individual
seeks to project himself out of the mass of being. But for Tutuola
the sense of disorder is horrifying: existence outside the relatedness of the human community is an existence in which there is
the stench of decay and death.

We shall have occasion later in this chapter to consider
whether Tutuola's picture of the Bush and of the boy-hero's
return from it reveal a penetration of the mythology of the old
Africa by Christian ideas and experience. For the moment, however, we shall turn to an author who presents a picture of the
old Africa which is very different from that of Tutuola. He is
a writer who would agree with Rousseau's famous dictum, 'Civili-

zation does not make men better, it makes them worse.' Camera
Laye focuses attention on the African judgment of the European
as one whose roots in the common soil of humanity have dried
up: in his novel *The Radiance of the King*[6] Laye presents
Africa as a spiritual refuge for a European who has lost the
basic shared joy of human life. The name of this man is Clarence. Without knowing why, he has come to a West African
country. He feels that he is searching for something which he
has failed to find in Europe. He has settled in an African town
where he lives in poverty and squalor, and is waiting there for
something to happen.

One day he sees a great crowd in the market-place and pushes
his way to the front. He is told that the King is coming – and
suddenly the King appears, riding along the road through the
town on a white horse. Clarence is astonished and overpowered
by the King's beauty. The King looks at Clarence, and Clarence
knows at once that this is why he has come to Africa – to see
the King. He must see him again, at whatever cost and even if
the quest takes his lifetime. He is told that the King will next
appear in a village far to the south, so in company with a beggar
and two boys Clarence sets off on the long journey. They spend
many months travelling through difficult country. The party
has to struggle through thick undergrowth and often seems
merely to be going round in circles. But at last they arrive and
Clarence settles in the village to await the coming of the King.
He waits there for the rest of his life. He has misgivings: perhaps the King will think he is unworthy and refuse to see him.
Perhaps he will not come at all. But Clarence waits, enjoying
in the meantime the secret favours of the local chief's harem,
whose members, to the chief's mild surprise, suddenly start
producing light-skinned children. When Clarence has almost
given up hope, the King appears, seated on a throne in the
market-place. Clarence stands watching him from a distance,
overwhelmed as before by his beauty. The King looks at him
and beckons. The King holds up his cloak and Clarence creeps
under it. And there, under the King's cloak, Clarence dies, but
his heart is full of joy and peace.

What we have in Camera Laye's story is the thesis that Europe must come to Africa to recover the innocence, the beauty, the humanity which she has lost. And she must come empty-handed and in humility, willing to share the basic toil and simplicity of African life without pretension and without losing heart. Her pilgrimage will be long, for Africa does not yield up her secrets to the casual visitor or the expatriate. The beauty of the King can be disclosed only to those who are willing to wait. But in the end the King *will* come, and he will wrap the European, alienated from his own humanity, in the folds of forgiveness.

Van der Post in *The Dark Eye in Africa* has said that he is old enough to remember the tremendous hope which dawned in Africa with the coming of the white man.[7] What we are beginning to see in some African literature today is a reversal of that hope. It is now Africa who is claiming to offer to Europe the spiritual assets whose loss is the price Europe has paid for her material advance. There is a conviction that Africa has preserved values which in Europe have been allowed to disintegrate. The European in Camera Laye's story is presented in sympathetic terms and without bitterness.* There is pity for the poor parlee-voo because he is seen as one who has become separated from the springs of life. A similar diagnosis is recorded by a former English missionary, John V. Taylor, in his book *The Primal Vision*.[8] While living in a Bugandan village, Taylor was troubled by insomnia so he consulted the local diviner about it. She said that his insomnia was caused by his refusal 'to bring the elders to completion, to discharge what the seniors require. It is his grandfather, his father and mother.' Taylor interpreted this to mean that he belonged to 'a generation whose roots had been attenuated and shrivelled': in this sense his parents *were* dead and the diviner had recognized his isolation.

It is interesting to notice that these claims for Africa are not being made only by African writers. There is also a Western nostalgia for the values, real or illusory, which Africa represents. Saul Bellow's novel, *Henderson the Rain King*, concerns a rough and tough American who finds in himself an undefined but deeply felt longing which nothing at home can fill.[9] He is a

---

* In saying this I dissent from the view of Ezekiel Mphahlele that Camera Laye presents Clarence 'with devastating irony'.

man of impulsive violence of whom his family and the neighbours go in considerable fear. He goes to Africa, and his whole
character changes profoundly. In a village, he discovers a small
tribe of tender-eyed people whose natural goodness extends in
sympathy even to their cattle which are dying of thirst because
the water-supply is polluted by frogs. The people mourn over
a dead animal as if it were a human being. Henderson is deeply
touched and is determined to help them. He contrasts the attitude of the Africans towards their cattle with his own brutal
indifference towards the pigs he used to rear. He decides to get
rid of the frogs by dynamiting them, but the charge is too
powerful and the water-supply is destroyed. Henderson's humili-
ation is complete, and he slips away from the village sadly aware
that his pride in American know-how was misplaced and that
the application of it has turned a crisis into a disaster.

Henderson's salvation, like that of Clarence, comes through
an African king. The King has had a Western education and
is, in fact, a far more literate man than Henderson; but he has
rejected the Western way of life and has returned to his tribe
over which he exercises a benevolent despotism. In all respects
except physical strength the King is Henderson's superior. It is
through the King that Henderson discovers that a man's fulfilment comes in the service of an ideal and the willingness to
offer oneself to life instead of fighting against it. Henderson is
aware that in the King there are spiritual depths which he himself does not possess, and his regard for the King develops to a
point which is not far short of worship. He has lost his soul
in Europe and America; but he has found it in Africa.

4

We may well feel that this 'Africa good, Europe bad' formula is
naïve and that European self-abasement before Africa is as inappropriate as European arrogance. If one thing is certain, it is
that, short of international catastrophe, the progress of material
development is irreversible and is already operating at a great
rate in many parts of Africa itself. In his book *Man in Rapid
Social Change*, Egbert de Vries has analysed the disruption of

traditional African life which the introduction of European methods has already caused.[10] This conflict between old and new, and the wedge which Westernization has thrust between the generations in Africa, is movingly and sometimes humorously realized in such novels as Achebe's *Things Fall Apart*,[11] T. M. Aluko's *One Man One Matchet*,[12] and Mongo Beti's *Mission to Kala*.[13] In spite of the claims being made by some writers for the old Africa, there does not appear to be any very convincing reason why Africa should succeed in preserving her deposit of communal values against erosion by individuating and differentiating forces. It is already fairly obvious that the European tide sweeps all before it, though it has now become indisputable that the Western democratic system is unable to harness traditional African loyalties and to create nationhood out of arbitrary groupings. Aimé Césaire is right in thinking that no political system, however admirable, can work if it is alien to the inherited wisdom of the people. The dilemma of independent Africa lies in the fact that the inherited wisdom has not the resources to deal with the economic and social complexities of a modern state.

Camera Laye's portrait of Clarence is a portrait, not only of the alienated European, but of the alienated African as well. If it were a question of choosing between traditional African culture and European material advancement, it is not hard to guess on which side the African choice would lie. Indeed, it can be said that the choice (if that is not an inappropriate word) has already been made, and that there is therefore something artificial in the promotion of the old Africa as a biddable option today. As James Baldwin has said, the one thing the African writer fails to explain is himself. He is already half Europeanized, and the nostalgia he expresses, the claims he makes for the old Africa, are possible only because he is himself posted at the European standpoint. In this connection, we have noticed that the writers who have been most emphatic in the search for Négritude have been those whose contact with the continent of Africa has been minimal; one suspects that what their work is really celebrating is not the loss of Africa but the fall of man.

I believe that there is one respect in which some African

writers have allowed themselves to be influenced by their European counterparts disastrously and unnecessarily. I refer to the elimination of religious values, the acceptance of a secular-materialist culture. One would have thought that such separation of culture from belief was highly *un*characteristic of the very 'Africanness' which the African writer wants to assert and explore, and that his absorption of European secularism had disqualified him for his self-chosen task.

This point was made in a paper read to the International Congress of Africanists[14] by the artist Elimo P. Njau,* who said, 'Most of them (artists and musicians of Africa today) appreciate the past African heritage in the arts and music. But they refuse to see the religious or spiritual background and the faith which brought these works of art into being. They refuse to see or cannot see this because they don't believe in God. They believe in themselves and individual freedom without direction. They create their works at random.' Those were strong and, in the atmosphere of an international congress, brave words. Njau was not asking his colleagues to recover their belief in the detailed spirit-world of their fathers; but he *was* asking them to believe in God. 'True art,' he said, 'grows from the soil and the full community that we live in. But where is the community? This is what we must create. How can we create it? Before we can create it we must create a new philosophy and a new understanding of God.'

Njau's thesis may be summarized thus:

1. The artistic creation of the old Africa grew out of the close-knit community of tribal life.
2. The cohesive power of that community was not only kinship but also shared belief in a spirit-world.
3. Community and shared belief have now disintegrated.
4. But the artist still needs community from which to draw inspiration. It must be recreated.
5. Such recreation is possible only on a basis of shared belief. A new understanding of God, freed from the old fears, is therefore needed.

* Njau is a Tanzanian and is now teaching art at Makerere University in Uganda.

6. This new understanding will imply the unity of all mankind, within which there will be differentiations and special insights.
7. African art will contribute to the unity of man through its expression of 'God's full presence in Africa'.

While losing nothing of its Africanness, Njau wants to see African art within the totality of the human vision. That vision is, for him, inseparable from faith in Jesus Christ. He believes that African art has a special contribution to make to the world-wide sharing of that vision and that faith; he believes in a God who makes every person and every thing unique and yet includes them all in the unity of his own being. Community will again be possible when men discover the God who, liberating them from the fears and provincialism of the past, gives that power of being which draws diversity into unity and overcomes man's alienation from the ground of his common humanity.

That striking phrase of Njau, 'individual freedom without direction', defines the attitude which some African writers seem to have learnt from those of Europe. It brings us back again to the inadequacy of the Sartrian estimate and reminds us of the weakness of any case which rests itself upon freedom without participation and responsibility. If the problem for Europe is that of finding a pattern of community which is capable of holding within itself the tensions of individual differentiation, the problem of Africa is to admit differentiation without destroying community. Perhaps it was of this that Césaire was thinking when he said that Africa need not follow the same path of evolution as Europe. Africa may yet prove that she can avoid the European blunders and achieve material advance without suffering the European loss of humanity.

For Njau, however, 'humanity' does not mean only the African humanity of Négritude: it means the universal humanity of Jesus Christ. John V. Taylor has said that when our eyes are aligned with the primal vision, which is the vision of Africa, 'it is supremely as the Second Adam that we see him (Christ) matching perfectly the needs and aspirations of that world'.[15] This is surely what we see in the discernment of Njau: he recognizes the solidarity of the human race in Jesus Christ – the calling and election of God which is grounded, not in the collective or the national, but in the personal, and must therefore become, as Kenneth Cragg says, 'a thesis of identity open to all peoples'.*

The Christ-figure appears in African literature predominantly as one who dispels divisive fears and hatreds and reconstitutes community. When he returns to his village after his long adventures in the Bush, the boy-hero of *My Life in the Bush of Ghosts* tells his family that 'it is in the Bush of Ghosts the "fears", "sorrows", "difficulties", all kind of the "punishments" etc. start and there they end'. He refers to an incident in an earlier novel of Tutuola, *The Palm Wine Drinkard*,[16] when the 'drinkard' and his wife are taken inside the 'White-tree'. Before entering the tree, the couple sell their death to somebody at the door and lend their fear to somebody else at the door. The result of these transactions is that 'we did not care about death and we did not fear again'. Inside the 'White-tree', the drinkard and his wife are welcomed by 'Faithful-Mother' who takes them into a large dancing hall where they find their own 'images' (perhaps large photographs are meant) which Faithful-Mother tells them are 'for remembrance and to know those she was helping from their difficulties and punishments'. The hall is beautifully decorated and there is continuous music and dancing. In the kitchen there are 'about three hundred and forty cooks', and there is also a hospital where patients are treated after their hardships in the Bush.

No doubt the White-tree has much in common with the paradisal dreams which are to be found in nearly all mythologies, and it may be quite unnecessary to bring in Christian ideas in order to explain it. But Amos Tutuola *is* a Christian, and it may not be going beyond the evidence to suggest that his story owes something to Christian influence. For example, one notices that the dancing hall, the kitchen and the hospital come not from mythological but from modern Africa, and that there is much in the dream to remind one of African Church life and festivals. Above all, it is hard not to see a hint of the presence of Christ the Redeemer in the two anonymous persons who buy

* See Kenneth Cragg's book *The Privilege of Man* (Athlone Press, London 1968), especially the chapter entitled 'The Chosen and the Nations'.

and borrow death and fear, by means of which the drinkard and his wife, who have been pursued and persecuted in the Bush, are admitted into an existence where communal values are realized. At least it can be said that here, in the idea that the Bush contains *within itself* the place of redemption, we are well inside the Christian circle of understanding.

The hero of *My Life in the Bush of Ghosts* is also essentially a redeemer. He passes through the place of disorder and death whose presence penetrates the living, human world and disrupts community. He passes through, maintaining his courage, his resourcefulness and his curiosity. He has descended into hell and risen from the dead, and he returns to his village as a liberator armed with saving knowledge. Fear, hatred and death have been defeated: new possibilities of freedom and participation have been opened up. The abyss has been plumbed and confronted.

Again, without wishing to make unsubstantiated claims, one may doubt whether Tutuola's story could have been written without the Christian Gospel. And it may be that the greatness of Africa will yet be disclosed, not in her Négritude, but in her power of response to the New Man in Christ. It may be that the radiance of the king, the radiance of the old 'primal' Africa, will become the radiance of the Christ of Africa, and that the Clarences of the future will turn to Africa to see his light and receive his reconciliation.

> One night in Galilee,
> You put hard fisherman's hands
> Into the spotless hands of artists,
> And at once a countless host of brothers
> From the rushes of the Nile
> To the steppes of Araby
> Found a light to guide them on their way,
> Through the mere beckoning of your finger.
>
> The world is on the brink of a new birth.
> We yearn for Passovers,
> Last Suppers and Wedding Feasts,
> Where meat and fish and wine
> Shall circle freely round the festive board
> And each shall have his fill.[17]

Notes

1. *Introduction à l'Anthologie de la nouvelle poésie nègre et Malagache*, Presses Universitaires. Reprinted in *Situations III*, Gallimard, Paris 1949, p. 237.

2. Max Warren, *The Missionary Movement from Britain in Modern History*, SCM Press, London 1965.

3. A. Césaire, *Lettre à Maurice Thorez*, Présence Africaine, Paris, 1956.

4. See the 'Report' by J. Baldwin in *Nobody Knows my Name*, Michael Joseph, London 1964 and Dial Press, New York 1961.

5. A. Tutuola, *My Life in the Bush of Ghosts*, Faber & Faber, London 1954 and Grove Press, New York 1954.

6. C. Laye, *The Radiance of the King*, Collins, London 1956.

7. Laurens van der Post, *The Dark Eye in Africa*, Hogarth Press, London 1955 and William Morrow, New York 1955.

8. John V. Taylor, *The Primal Vision*, SCM Press, London 1963, pp. 148-50 and Fortress Press, Philadelphia.

9. S. Bellow, *Henderson the Rain King*, Weidenfeld and Nicolson, London 1959, Penguin Books, 1966 and Viking Press, New York 1959.

10. E. de Vries, *Man in Rapid Social Change*, SCM Press, London 1961 and Doubleday & Co., Garden City 1961.

11. C. Achebe, *Things Fall Apart*, Heinemann, London 1958.

12. T. M. Aluko, *One Man One Matchet*, Heinemann, London 1964 and Lawrence Verry, Conn. 1965.

13. M. Beti, *Mission to Kala*, Heinemann, London 1958.

14. *Proceedings of the First International Congress of Africanists*, Longmans, Green & Co., London 1964.

15. John V. Taylor, *op. cit.*, pp. 124-5.

16. A. Tutuola, *The Palm Wine Drinkard*, Faber & Faber, London 1952.

17. Camille Roussan, *Christ*, quoted by B. B. Dadie, tr. C. L. Patterson, in *Proceedings etc.*

5

The Sisyphean Hero

Among post-war writers in Europe who, while sharing to the full in the 'absurdist' experience of a Sartre, have nevertheless succeeded in giving shape to a human protest which is both individual and corporate, the name of Albert Camus stands high. His famous novel *The Plague* has a quality of moral affirmation which lifts it above the negativities of mere nihilism and imparts to it a tragic grandeur.

The Mediterranean 'climate' of much of the work of Camus, with its delight in sea and sun and its enjoyment of human beauty, has reminded some readers of Ancient Greece. There is also more than a suggestion of Greek drama in his most important writing, and his thought is easier to grasp if we look first at his essay entitled *Le Mythe de Sisyphe*.[1]

The gods condemned Sisyphus to roll a rock to the top of a mountain from which the rock immediately rolled down to the bottom and the laborious toil had to begin again. As Camus says, the gods 'rightly thought that there is no punishment more terrible than work which is useless and without hope'. The moments of greatest interest in the labour of Sisyphus are those in which he walks down the mountain after his rock. What are his thoughts? These are his moments of reflection – this hour which is like a respite is the time in which Sisyphus thinks about his destiny. And because of this power of thought he is stronger than his rock. It is the human capacity for reflection that enables us to recognize our destiny as tragic; yet in the midst of this tragedy there is also joy. The rock is Sisyphus' rock and he has the power to seize his destiny and make it his own. He marches down the mountain with heavy, measured tread towards the torment that has no end. But 'the struggle to the summit is enough of itself to fill a man's heart. It is necessary to imagine that Sisyphus was happy.'

Here, then, we have a curious paradox. The existence of man is absurd – even man himself is absurd – and yet his ability to pass this judgment is a cause of joy for it proves that he is greater than his meaningless destiny. We are reminded here of the famous passage in Pascal's *Pensées* about the 'thinking reed'. 'It is not from space that I must seek my dignity,' says Pascal, 'but from the government of my thought. I shall have no more if I possess worlds. By space the universe encompasses and swallows me up like an atom; by thought I comprehend the world.' The judgment of man's consciousness, as Camus points out in *The Rebel*,[2] can be extended even to death, which seems to make indifference the final word. Sacrificial death, so far from being the ultimate absurdity, is the demonstration of freedom and the creation of 'honour'. 'Kaliayev climbs the gallows and visibly designates to all his fellow-men the exact limit where the honour of man begins and ends.'*

For Camus, the greatness of man, that which releases him from absurdity, lies in his 'consciousness' and his power of rebellion – a rebellion which Camus calls 'metaphysical'. It is a rebellion, not so much against the terms in which existence is given, as against the submissiveness, the unthinking acceptance, which allows those terms to determine human reality. This Sisyphean theme is the basis of Camus' novel, *The Plague*,[3] which could be said to be an extended working out, in a modern setting, of the old myth.

2

The story tells of an outbreak of bubonic plague in the North African town of Oran. It begins among the rats, but rapidly spreads to the people until a state of emergency has to be declared and the town gates are locked. No one may enter or leave

* *The Rebel*, p. 253. Camus is referring to the Russian terrorist who murdered the Grand Duke Sergei in 1905. This is the subject of his play, *Les Justes*. The point is that the rebel is prepared to *give* his life, whereas the revolutionary will only *risk* it.

– the inhabitants are forced into a Sisyphean drama, from which there is no escape.

The plague itself is open to a number of possible explanations. There is little doubt that a parallel can be drawn between the situation in Oran and that of German-occupied France from 1940 to 1945, during which period in fact Camus started to write his novel. But as Philip Thody points out, 'it would be limiting to see *La Peste* as the description of a particular historical experience . . . it opens out into a much wider context'.[4] What Camus seems to have in mind is the Sisyphean nature of human existence itself.* The human struggle never ends because there is no power to enter the world from outside, no *deus ex machina*, to call a halt to the conditions in which the only meaningful option is the rebellion against them. The plague, as Camus tells us at the end of the novel, is never finally conquered.

> Rieux remembered . . . that the plague bacillus never dies or disappears for good; that it can lie dormant for years and years in furniture and linen-chests; that it bides its time in bedrooms, cellars, trunks, and bookshelves; and that perhaps the day would come when, for the bane and enlightening of men, it roused up its rats again and sent them forth to die in a happy city (p. 252).

The detailed horror of the plague is movingly realized by Camus. The disease falls upon the town apocalyptically, disclosing by its own monstrous senselessness the far less obvious but no less senseless character of the everyday existence of its citizens. The plague does not destroy meaning: it reveals meaninglessness as already present in the banal routines of work and pleasure. There is a man trying to write a novel who has produced only the first sentence which he constantly revises. There is another man whose spare-time occupation is to stand on the balcony of his house and spit at cats in the street below. These men are living a Sisyphean existence *but they do not recognize it*, and the same is true of the vast majority of the citizens of Oran. Only *consciousness*, says Camus in *Le Mythe de Sisyphe*, can reveal the tragedy and the joy secreted in absurdity, and only the rebellion which follows from this recognition can force

---

* In *Le Mythe de Sisyphe*, Camus mentions the modern working man's repetitive labour and calls Sisyphus 'the proletarian of the gods'. Another person whose work is markedly Sisyphean is, of course, the housewife.

meaning into solid, recognizable form. The people of Oran hope
foolishly for a remission of the plague or for escape from it:
they have failed to realize that the plague is inherent in existence
itself, and that the only course open to man is to accept its
challenge and fight for his 'honour'.

There are, however, in Oran a small number of Sisyphean
heroes – men who are prepared to march down the mountain
with heavy, measured tread and prove that they are stronger
than the plague which destroys them. These are the men who
recognize absurdity and accept its conditions, but who fight it
relentlessly without expecting any absolute to vindicate or ter-
minate their struggle. There is the hero and narrator of the
story, Dr Rieux, who directs the medical operations and believes
that 'honesty consists in doing my job'. There is Tarrou, a man
who wants to be 'a saint without God', who organizes 'sanitary
squads' to patrol the streets and find victims of the disease.
There is Rambert, a journalist, who tries to escape from the
plague-stricken town to rejoin the woman he loves; but he decides
not to go, because 'it may be shameful to be happy by oneself'.
There is Othon, a stiff, unsympathetic magistrate, who, after his
little boy dies of the plague, volunteers to help in the isolation
camp. The greatness of man is revealed by these men: they
prove that 'there are more things in men to admire than to
despise'.

What, then, is the substance of this Camusian rebellion? Can
it be defined? There is a scene when an old man named Grand
is looking at a shop-window decorated for Christmas. He is
remembering his wife as a young girl in the early days of their
marriage before she left him. Rieux sees Grand but is himself
unnoticed.

And he knew, also, what the old man was thinking as his tears
flowed, and he, Rieux, thought it too: that a loveless world is
a dead world and always there comes an hour when one is weary
of prisons, of one's work, and of devotion to duty, and all one
craves for is a loved face, the warmth and wonder of a loving
heart . . . At this moment he suffered with Grand's sorrow, and
what filled his breast was the passionate indignation we feel when
confronted by the anguish all men share (pp. 213-14).

This passionate indignation is at the heart of the rebellion. It is
the sense of outrage one feels at the death in agony of a little
boy; it is the struggle to save a friend's life and the smile of
comradeship on his lips when, after all, he dies; it is recognition
of the harm human beings do to one another, because we are all
'plague-stricken' and we must try to infect as few people as
possible. Rebellion is also to go for a swim for friendship's sake,
'because really it's too damn silly living only in and for the
plague. Of course a man should fight for the victims, but, if
he ceases caring for anything outside that, what's the use of his
fighting?'* And the record of the plague, the account of it which
Rieux has written,

> could be only the record of what had had to be done, and what
> assuredly would have to be done again in the never-ending fight
> against terror and its relentless onslaughts, despite their personal
> afflictions, by all who, while unable to be saints but refusing to
> bow down to pestilences, strive their utmost to be healers
> (pp. 251-2).

Conquest of the absurd is found in the work of compassion –
the honour of man begins with his willingness to offer himself
in sacrificial death. But it also ends there, for there is nothing
beyond death to make the sacrifice permanently effective. The
pestilence always reasserts itself, the stone always rolls back down
the mountain, and we are 'toujours en marche'. The universe does
not resonate in tune with the actions of men and there are no
absolutes to exempt them from their endless struggle. Indeed,
absolutes are themselves principles of death. When men *act* in
the name of absolutes they soon forget that there is an inter-
mingling of evil with good in every human action, they forget
their own inescapable contingency, they forget 'la mesure'. They

---

* I find myself thinking here of the irony that, on the day after the
Russian invasion of Czechoslovakia, Rostropovitch was playing the
Dvořák cello concerto with the Russian State Orchestra in the Albert
Hall, London. There was some heckling from the audience, but not much.
The dominating feeling seemed to be that the music and the players
were expressing a universal humanity which was itself the most radical
criticism of tyranny. This was something outside the plague which
validated the human struggle and reminded us that there are still more
things in men to admire than to despise.

begin to regard *themselves* as absolutes, so that they murder in order to prevent murder, they commit acts of injustice in order to establish justice.

Equally, when men *submit* to absolutes the result is death. The priest in *The Plague* tells his congregation that 'plague is the flail of God and the world his threshing-floor'; man's part must therefore be to accept it as the divine judgment, to refuse the rebellion which questions the divine verdict, to submit to the sentence of God. The priest dies with his face to the wall having refused medical help. He dies in the terrible solitude of obedience to God. Perhaps it was not even the plague that killed him; perhaps he died simply because he gave in. Submission to the will of God means repudiation of human values – values which man, not God, creates; values which must constantly be recreated, for they 'are never given once for all and the fight to uphold them must go on unceasingly'. 'To leave all justice to God', says Camus in *The Rebel*, 'is to sanctify injustice', and that is why 'it is better to die on one's feet than live on one's knees'.

In the work of Camus, then, we see the human rebellion hurling itself against a meaningless universe and claiming for itself the power to justify happiness. The rebellion is not an individual act of Promethean defiance, but a work of human compassion, and it neither seeks nor requires any absolute to vindicate it. In the words of Colin Smith, 'Rebellion has its own meaning as the final action of which man is capable when everything else dissolves into irrationality and death.' The meaning is in the rebellion itself: it is not in the *results* of rebellion, which may be nothing but failure and which in any case can never create permanent values. All we know is that the irrational and deathly conditions which demand rebellion will never be other than they are, and that rebellion itself will always be the only way open to man to establish his 'honour'. This means that the fight must go on unceasingly: the honour of man is lost when he submits to the false absolutes of bourgeois morality or political or religious dogmas. It is also lost when he forgets his own profound implication in the deathly conditions against which he fights: for man is himself 'plague-stricken' and cannot help doing harm even when he would do good. He is bound to be a 'murderer'; the best he can do is to try to be an 'innocent murderer', one who at least does not do harm deliberately. This requires vigilance and clarity. Our involvement in tragic guilt is inescapable: even Christ, says Clamence in *The Fall*,[5] shared in it when the Innocents were slaughtered because of him, and perhaps Clamence is right when he says that the cry of Rachel weeping for her children rang for ever in his ears. So the rebellion is not much to set against the plague and the labour of Sisyphus; not much, but enough. It *must* be enough: 'it is necessary to imagine that Sisyphus was happy'.

3

The obvious difference between Camus and Sartre is that the former gives an important place to human relatedness and avoids the latter's loveless individualism. For both writers there can be only one kind of meaning, and that is the meaning created by man himself; but for Camus this meaning is found not so much in individual as in corporate action, and the metaphysical rebellion which he demands issues in a sense of human solidarity. This is the exit from absurdity: 'In absurdist experience suffering is individual. But from the moment that a movement of rebellion begins, suffering is seen as a collective experience – as the experience of everyone.'* Rebellion is 'the clue which lures the individual from his solitude . . . I *rebel* – therefore we *exist*'. In *The Plague*, this thesis is demonstrated most clearly by Othon, a magistrate. He has always been a cold, aloof man, regulating his life by principles rather than compassion. He suffers the terrible death of his little boy almost in silence: this is the experience of absurdity by which all principles are shattered and in which we are alone; but when Othon is sent to the isolation camp – it is a rule that all who have been in contact with a plague-victim must go into isolation for some weeks – he performs various menial tasks and soon becomes a useful member of the camp. He has now entered the ranks of the rebels, which

---

* *The Rebel*, p. 28. Raymond Williams argues that this move from individual to collective experience may be merely 'rhetorical' here, but is convincingly 'actual' in *The Plague*. See *Modern Tragedy*, pp. 181-2.

means that he has begun to recognize the corporate nature of
suffering and is exposed to human need. When he is discharged
from the camp, he asks Rieux if he can go back to work there –
and Rieux notices that there is 'a sudden gentleness in those
hard, inexpressive eyes'. It is thus the rebellion that draws man
out of his individual solitude and impels him towards others.
'The individual is not, in himself, an embodiment of the values
he wishes to defend. It needs at least all humanity to comprise
them.' Therefore the fact of rebellion implies the existence of a
human nature: 'why rebel if there is nothing worth preserving
in oneself?' Camus asks. Man does not begin, as he does in
Sartre, at the absolute zero of individual responsibility where he
must project himself out of the undefined mass of being; man for
Camus is one who has in him the power to rebel against the
absurdity of his existence, and Camus seems to imply that this
power is man's defining characteristic which makes it possible to
speak of a 'human nature'. I shall argue later that Camus does
not succeed in showing why this 'metaphysical' rebellion should
express itself in terms of compassion and sacrifice rather than
in terms of self-interest. For the moment, however, we notice
Camus' insistence that the power to rebel can all too easily be
lost when men simply accept the senselessness of their existence
in a universe which offers them nothing but disorder and outrage.
To abdicate from the rebellion against such a universe is to lose
one's manhood – to become inhuman.

We must remember, however, that the rebellion contains no
absolute to make human action unambiguous or to create conditions from which absurdity is banished. The values we seek
are found in the act of rebellion itself: once they are erected into
an ideology, once they take the form of an End which is thought
to be independent of human action and capable of automatic
realization – then they cease to be human values and become
instead the cause of inhuman tyranny or of indifference towards
the concrete needs of suffering humanity. It is on these grounds
that Camus rejects Christianity, with which, at first sight, his
understanding has so much in common. He points out that
'there is an act of metaphysical rebellion at the beginning of
Christianity', – by which, presumably, he means the cross of

Christ. We have already noticed the view of Camus that a man's offering of himself in sacrificial death is the only way by which he can establish his 'honour'; it is a 'metaphysical' victory because in fact the absurdity of death *is* the final word and the joy which can be wrested out of this tragic destiny does not alter its inevitability or make it any the less absurd. But Camus parts company with the Christian scheme when it asserts the resurrection of Christ and announces the kingdom of Heaven. These dogmas, he says, render the cross 'futile'. This conclusion will not surprise us if we have followed the Camusian repudiation of 'absolutes'. To put it into traditional terms, Camus cannot subscribe to any 'objective' theory of the atonement: the cross is meaningful because it typifies the human rebellion against the senselessness of existence, but we make a serious mistake if we think that it has created new conditions in which meaning has somehow become 'given' and permanent. This is precisely the mistake which the Church *has* made. If there is resurrection, if a supernatural order has now imposed its solutions upon absurdity, then Christ's death is no longer the desperate throw of man against futility; it is surrender, not rebellion, and it is therefore 'inhuman' in the sense that it ends by denying the need for rebellion and proclaims acceptance as the way of salvation. So man loses one of his essential dimensions, and turns into an ideology the values which have no existence except in unceasing, ever-renewed struggle.

Camus distinguishes sharply between 'the only two possible worlds that can exist for the human mind': they are 'the world of grace' and 'the rebel world'.[6] The former is Christian, the latter is not. Either we deny all power to justify ourselves and wait submissively for supernatural blessings; or we decide that meaning can come only from our own efforts, and act accordingly. The priest, Paneloux, in *The Plague*, believes in the world of grace even though the fact of human suffering refutes its existence: the doctor, Rieux, fights against the plague without belief – simply because that is where 'honesty' leads. The result is that Paneloux passes more and more deeply into solitude while Rieux finds in himself an increasing identification with others. And this is the criterion by which rebellion is to be judged –

whether or not it succeeds in creating human solidarity. It is true that rebellion can be lost or distorted 'through lassitude or folly', and then it becomes 'an accomplice to murder'; absurdity is fundamentally the denial of love, and the rebel must maintain perpetual vigilance lest he 'fasten infection' on others and thus become an instrument of the very absurdity against which he fights. But the Christian has lost this fight before he even begins. His beliefs lead him along one of two courses: either he seeks to impose his 'absolutes' upon others and thus becomes a tyrant, forgetting that he is himself not an absolute but a pestiferous human being; or he submits tamely to absurdity and tries to assure himself that suffering will have its compensation in eternal life, thus despairing of present human transcendence and passing by the healing task in which men find unity.

4

One sometimes feels with Camus, as one does with Sartre, that the writer's theory fails to give an adequate account of his own artistic creation. Is it really possible for man to fight for ever in a hopeless war? Has not Camus turned absurdity itself into an absolute? Is it necessary to assert categorically that there is no meaning except what man creates? or that belief in 'resurrection' makes the human rebellion futile? Does not Camus fail to answer the crucial question – why should man be a rebel at all if there is nothing outside himself by which his actions may be supported? If the existence of all objective moral values is denied, it is hard to see how we can fail to arrive at a totally nihilistic conclusion. As it is, in Camus one suspects the presence of a categorical imperative in rebellion itself: we rebel, not to assert values and not to claim solidarity with other men – for it is only when we have *begun* to rebel that these products reveal themselves; we rebel simply because we must. But why must we? Is it really possible to accept Rieux's explanation that he is simply 'doing his job'? What is it that prompts a man to stay with the victims of the plague – why should he seek to be a true healer, at the cost, it may be, of his own life, against the strong instinct of self-preservation? Even Rambert, the self-centred journalist, whose only thought is to escape from the plague-stricken town in order that he may rejoin the woman he loves – even Rambert finally recognizes an imperative in the claims of the victims and decides to stay. Decisions like this are really as absurd and inexplicable as the plague itself. But Rieux, after an initial moment of surprise, accepts Rambert's decision in a matter-of-fact way which, one feels, is something less than adequate to its extraordinariness. One would have expected him to take less for granted this evidence of self-denying values in man. But we know that Camus has decided that he must avoid any hint of imperatives which might imply some kind of *religious* interpretation of human awareness. Only absurdity can safely be absolutized because only a very few religious fanatics, like Paneloux, can persuade themselves that the Absurd is God. The rest is relative and impermanent; and it can never win.

But there is much of the work of Camus to which the appropriate response is one of gratitude. *The Plague* is one of those rare novels which release the tragic protest and deepen our awareness of what is 'genuinely human'. We recognize ourselves in it, and yet we did not know that we could be as admirable as this. Given the conditions of the plague, we might all hope to act like a Rieux or a Tarrou or an Othon.

Camus is surely right in thinking that to understand oneself as 'genuinely human' is to understand oneself as a rebel. It is important, however, to remove political overtones from the word 'rebel'. While it is true that the human rebellion may and often will find political forms of expression, the 'metaphysical' rebellion of which Camus speaks refers to something which pre-exists specific forms of rebellion and stands for a characteristic of our existential awareness as such. The word is not used to mean an attempt to overthrow some constituted authority: it points rather to the vision, the questioning, the *protest* which man finds in himself. The starting-point of rebellion is the recognition that the world provides no objective correlate which is coincident with man's interior vision, and it lays upon him the necessity of acting in the light of that vision while refusing to be an instrument of the forces which threaten it. For Camus, the human struggle lies in the attempt to create order and meaning under the overarching absurdity of the universe. Principally, this is the work of alleviating suffering and of refusing to be a carrier of the plague-germ; it is the willingness to give one's life for others and to decline escape-routes; and it must never become an attempt to impose some absolutist programme upon other people.

In the sense in which Camus uses the term, we would all be proud to be called 'rebels', though we might have to admit that it is a hard vocation and that we seldom live up to it. Most of us are so busy trying to adjust ourselves to the changes and complexities of modern life that we seem to have little energy for rebellion; a letter to *The Times* is hardly at the level of heroism which Camus requires, and we can nearly always find reasons for thinking that conformity is the highest virtue in most areas of work and service. It could be argued that, for many of us, absurdity comes not through apocalyptic events but through the very systems by which we try to control and ease our existence. We shall have occasion to think about this when we look at the novels of Kafka. For the moment, however, let us see whether we can agree with Camus that rebellion *is* an essential dimension in our self-understanding and that the sickness of our age lies in our failure to maintain the interior vision out of which it springs.

It could be that our rebellion is a consequence of our *fallen* nature and that we would make a serious mistake if we held it to be characteristic of true humanity. We notice that there is no instance in the Old Testament where the verb 'rebel' and its cognates is used in anything other than a bad sense. Most of the uses of the word refer to rebellion against God. For the OT writers, rebellion is precisely that which introduces disorder and misery into human affairs: it is the 'stiff-necked' and 'gainsaying' attitude which refuses the God who stretches out his hands to his people. Clearly, rebellion against God is not a virtue, and out of this general conviction the view could develop that *any* rebellion of man against the conditions of his life must be understood as defiance of the God who is alone responsible for those conditions and who 'unites in himself absolute power with absolute justice, goodness, and wisdom'.* Thus Jephthah's daughter submissively accepts her fate as the divine will, and Job's protests are silenced by the inscrutable majesty of the Creator.

This view is very close to that of the priest in *The Plague*, but Camus is wrong in thinking that it is Christian. Even in the OT there is plenty of evidence for belief in the share of man in the creation of meanings and in the improvement of the conditions of his life. Of course man falls into disaster and ridicule when he thinks he knows better than God: how can he pit himself against the Lord of the whole earth without presumption? But the God he serves is not an inscrutable tyrant. He declares his purpose through his servants the prophets and invites the partnership of man in his actions. It is true that events may often seem to be contrary to the divine purpose and the conditions of life may sometimes appear intractable, but the faith of the OT is the faith that God is present in bad times as well as good, and that the frustration of his purposes is due not to his own failure but to that of his human agents. Of course there are limits to human understanding beyond which God *is* inscrutable and his ways past tracing out; if this were not so, God would be nothing more than an idol – a projection of human fantasies and ambitions claiming authoritative status. But the prophets of Israel will have none of this. The divine word is not an echo of human ambitions: it is a word of judgment as well as promise; it summons men to depart from iniquity and to ally themselves with the divine compassion.

There are thus two kinds of rebellion open to man: the false, self-destroying kind which is rebellion *against* God; and the true, liberating and life-giving kind which is rebellion *with* God. To obey God is to become a rebel against sin and evil, against all that separates man from the source of life and virtue, against all the destructive forces inside and outside man which masquerade as God. To obey God is also to align oneself with meanings and values which have their source in God but which

* I am referring here to an article in *The Listener* (September 2, 1955) by D. Daiches Raphael entitled *Tragedy and Religion*. He argues that tragedy depends upon the human rebellion and is therefore incompatible with 'the religion of the Bible'.

man himself is called to actualize in human history – in politics, economics, social organization, as well as in the individual himself. The fact that these meanings and values always transcend the power of man to grasp or achieve is the reason why the human rebellion always has a Sisyphean character and never attains finality; at the same time, it also forces upon man the realization that he is not God. Only a transcendent God can give the lie to the absolutist claims of man; only a transcendent God is our safeguard against attributing divine authority to human programmes. Camus is right when he points to the terrible consequences which follow when man introduces 'absolutes' into his affairs and claims to be acting in their name.* But this is precisely the primal sin of man in the biblical doctrine: 'ye shall be as gods' are the words which lead to the Fall; it is man at the height of his aspiration who forgets the limits of rebellion and plunges into disorder and misery. But without the transcendent God to remind him of his imperfect insights and the hidden 'cellarage' of his self-regard, there is no reason why he should ever do otherwise or understand the cause of his collapse.

The transcendence of God is therefore both the source of the human rebellion and its limitation. It is the source because man finds himself grasped by a power other than himself and in touch with values which are independent of his own projects: it is the limitation because the very values which summon him to rebellion also reveal the ambiguity of his motives and the inadequacy of his achievement. Man is neither the passive recipient of imposed meanings nor the inventor of all the meaning there is.† In the secular order he is an 'applied scientist' whose job is to actualize in human life at every level the truths which have their origin in God, but without supposing that either his knowledge of those truths or its application is final.

---

* Compare Simone Weil: 'We must always be prepared to change sides with Justice – that fugitive from the winning camp.'

† Here I dissent from Harvey Cox, *The Secular City*, SCM Press, 1965, p. 72.

5

It is clear that Jesus was himself a 'rebel', and if proof were needed that rebellion is characteristic of what is genuinely human, then surely it is here. Of course, to call Jesus a rebel is to apply to him a word which neither the NT nor the Church uses of him: apart from its almost inescapable political resonances, the word perhaps implies a certain immaturity as of a young man asserting his independence. But we have seen that the Camusian meaning is very different. To be a rebel is to live by an interior vision, a categorical imperative, which refuses to bow down to pestilences and demands that men shall be healers. In this sense, Jesus was the greatest of all rebels. The point need not be laboured: the works of healing and feeding, the refusal to coerce, the willingness to die – all are evident in the gospels. It is not surprising that there is much in *The Plague* to remind us of Christ; indeed, one feels that Camus was somewhat haunted by the gospel Figure even though he had to repudiate Christian theology.

In the preface to the American edition of his earlier novel, *The Outsider*, Camus remarked that its hero, Meursault, was 'the only kind of Christ we deserve'.[7] This was no doubt a deliberately provocative statement – Camus admits that he speaks with a certain irony – but the hint is certainly worth following up. At first sight it is not easy to see Meursault as a Christ-figure even in an ironical sense. He is characterized by 'a complete indifference to anything except immediate physical sensations, together with an absolute refusal to lie about his own emotions' (Thody). What Camus has in mind in his half-identification of Meursault with Christ is perhaps his silence before his judges, his refusal to plead for acquittal in a way which would endorse the false bourgeois morality in the light of which the trial is conducted. Meursault is accused of shooting an Arab, which indeed he had done in a moment of half-consciousness when he was blinded by the sun, but it is not so much because of the deed that he is condemned to death as because of the complete indifference he displays during his trial. He is a man who is intensely in love with life, especially in the physical sensations

produced by light and colour and movement, but he stands
outside all the normal structures of social relatedness and the
moral values by which they are sustained. Meursault had not
wept at his mother's funeral; he had refused promotion at work;
he had had no feelings of romantic love for Marie, his girl-
friend; he showed no remorse over his killing of the Arab. He
is condemned because he is callous, indifferent, and contemptu-
ous. The trial simply fails to touch his central being.

Meursault understands himself and his life in terms which
are entirely foreign to the conventional outlook of his judges.
He cannot defend himself without expressing a sorrow he does
not feel, and to express such sorrow would be to play the bourgeois game of pretending that life has meaning and that the
authorities know what it is. But Meursault is the 'absurd man'
of *Le Mythe de Sisyphe* who knows that there are no meanings
and who sees through the pretence and hypocrisy of official
morality. It is in the light of this detached interior conviction
that Meursault faces his judges and finally prepares to climb
the scaffold. He is prepared to die for the sake of the truth. He
resembles Christ in his silent rejection of the official *mores* at his
trial and in the condemnation which rejection brings upon
himself. He is, in short, a 'metaphysical rebel' who chooses 'the
benign indifference of the universe' just as Sisyphus 'chooses'
his rock and Rieux 'chooses' the plague – because that is where
honesty leads. The destiny of the outsider is to be condemned
and by his condemnation to reveal the corruption of consciousness in the human system by which he is judged. Meursault
and the other Camusian heroes 'choose' an absurdity by which
all human systems are revealed as lies. Christ chooses the cross,
with similar effect. But there is one great difference. The choice
of Meursault leaves us with absurdity as the final word, whereas
the choice of Christ reaches out to a meaning beyond absurdity
by which the tragic worth of our mundane existence is affirmed.

For Meursault is a Christ *manqué*, the only Christ we deserve.
Camus cannot accept the belief that Christ has defeated absurdity and has decisively altered the conditions in which the human
struggle takes place. It may indeed seem impossible to combine
the human rebellion with obedience to a divine will and to claim

that the work of Christ has a finality which is denied to ours. Yet we have to assert about Jesus two seemingly contradictory truths: that he thought and acted in terms of an absolute and referred his own will to that of the heavenly Father; and that his life was characterized, as ours is, by responsibility, by doubt, inner conflict, and the final absurdity of death. 'Him who knew no sin,' said St Paul, 'God made to be sin on our behalf,'[8] pointing us to the solution of the difficult problem of how the truth of God can be actualized within the Sisyphean existence of man without the imposition of an absolute which would bring the human rebellion to an end.

6

The answer, I believe, is to be found by considering the nature of the divine absolute which Jesus embodied and actualized. That absolute is love, and in understanding this we are at once removing from our thought any notion of coercion or violence or arbitrariness. For love is characterized, not by any exercise of arbitrary power, nor by the imposition of rules or formulas, but by the very opposite of all this – by self-giving, by identification, by acceptance of responsibility for human suffering. As Berdyaev has said, God has not even the power of a gendarme: his power towards men is of a different order from that of coercive authority. It follows that love is present only where there *is* self-giving and participation with others, and this means that not even God can create conditions in which love works like a computer carrying out a programmed operation. The human rebellion is not made superfluous by Christ: on the contrary, it is underwritten and reinforced. Christ has shown that we do not fight in darkness and isolation, but as it were in company with God himself. The resurrection does not make our rebellion 'futile' as Camus says: to say that it does is to regard it as an act of arbitrary power by a god from the machine. But Christians do not think of the resurrection as an eleventh-hour retrieval of disaster: it is understood as the culmination of the love of Christ, the proof that his way is the authentic way and that reality endorses it. From Christ we learn that rebellion *is* the

only way open to man to establish his 'honour', and at the same
time we discover that the Sisyphean cycle has been broken.
The war is not hopeless. The honour of man begins on a cross
but it does not end there, for the values actualized by Christ
within the human context have been taken into the divine
context and stamped with an eternal guarantee. The interior
vision of man is matched and transcended by the actuality of
Christ; the absolute is not absurdity but love, and the strange
work of love overcomes absurdity.

> For the creation was subjected to vanity . . . in hope that the
> creation itself also shall be delivered from the bondage of corrup-
> tion into the liberty of the glory of the children of God.

I think we must say that Camus is mistaken when he places
in opposition to each other the world of grace and the rebel world.
To live by grace is to live as a 'rebel' and to find one's power of
rebellion increased. This may seem a startling statement to
those who see in the Church nothing but submission and in-
action, but I agree with Harvey Cox in his belief that it is one of
the great biblical correctives to the distortions of 'tradition'.
Catholic and Protestant alike have too often understood 'grace'
or 'justification' in essentially *static* terms having little to do
with the ongoing challenge of the secular conditions of man's
existence. This is not to deny the Church's historic role in the
relief of need and suffering, but generally speaking this role has
been performed without much radical questioning by the Church
of the political, social, and economic orders themselves.* But
twentieth-century man has become convinced that there is a
human duty to contrive changes in these orders for the betterment of human life,† and this discovery has brought under

* Commenting on the attitude of the early Christians to the Roman
civilization around them, F. R. Barry says, 'The existing structures of
human life – rich and poor, masters and slaves – were just there, whether
so ordained by God's creation or, as Christian theology was to suggest
later, permitted as consequences of the Fall. They made no attempt to
alter or reform them'. *Christian Ethics and Secular Society*, p. 114,
Hodder & Stoughton, 1966. The whole chapter on 'The Christian Society'
may be consulted.

† This, of course, goes back at least as far as nineteenth-century
Comtism.

question the Church's 'metaphysical' understanding of salvation as a 'state of grace' defined by its detachment from and therefore its essential *acquiescence in* the secular orders of existence. This is, of course, part of the Camusian case against Christianity – that it leads men to abdicate from the human duty of rebellion in favour of meanings and values which are prefabricated and other-worldly, with the corollary that life on earth is something to be endured rather than improved and enjoyed. There is, no doubt, such a thing as Christian fortitude when circumstances cannot be altered, but Camus is undoubtedly right in thinking that fortitude must not be allowed to become a total substitute for rebellion. To borrow van Buren's metaphor, when there is a fire at sea the important thing is not to try to understand oneself as a man on board a burning ship but to put the fire out.[9] Modern man has come to the conclusion that if God is to be found at all he is to be found in the secular meanings and challenges which confront him in the actualities of his existence. The theological case for this view has been argued by a good number of contemporary theologians, among them Harvey Cox whose stimulating book *The Secular City*[10] shows how much modern biblical scholarship has contributed to this more pragmatic type of religious awareness. The Christian Faith is seen not so much as the guarantee of eternal salvation but rather as the charter for human action by which man is liberated for secular programmes and invited to collaborate with God and his fellow-men in the better ordering of life. There is no difficulty in showing that this understanding has biblical support; but it is not the whole story.

7

The trouble with 'correctives' is that they usually correct too much and end up as substitutes. Biblical understanding does not require us to choose between grace and rebellion; nor does it require us to abandon belief in metaphysical values which pre-exist human programmes and give them direction and impetus. To live by grace in the NT sense is to be seized by a power which forces men out of their self-centred prisons into the world of sin and suffering and need where Christ himself operated – a power which, at least in some measure, reproduces the victorious rebellion of Christ. Let us concede that the Church has not always exhibited this power, that it has too often been concerned only with the perpetuation of its own existence, and has, as Berdyaev says, attempted to live by law rather than by the creative energy of the Spirit.* Against this betrayal of its origins the emphasis today on secular action is a recovery by the Church of New Testament truth. But it is not true that we discover the meanings and values by which we ought to live only as we take up the secular challenge: if this were so, there would be no sufficient reason for taking up the challenge at all. As Tillich points out,[11] dynamics without form drives man in all directions without any definite aim and content, and the drive is likely to be, not towards the secular challenge, but towards the preoccupations of self-interest. On the other hand, to take some kind of form *out* of the dynamics in which it occurs and then impose it on dynamics to which it does not belong is to act in terms of an absolute which, as Camus has warned us, is destructive and deathly. But the NT does not offer us either of these alternatives: it offers us Jesus Christ and the creative life of the Spirit – and if we may continue with Tillich's terminology, Jesus is the *form* and the Spirit is the *dynamics* of the Christian life. But to refer to Christ as 'form' is, we believe, to make an assertion not only about the human context but also about the *divine* context, and this means that there is a permanence, a transcendence about Christ which places him 'beyond, behind, and above the passing flux of things' (Whitehead) and makes him a source of meanings and values relevant to but not limited by our partial, finite perspectives. To speak of the Holy Spirit as 'dynamics' is to assert the working out, the incarnation of those meanings and values in the contemporary human context. In other words, there is both a givenness and a potentiality in Christian faith, both the permanent achievement of Christ and the potential actualization of that achievement by

* *Spirit and Reality*. Berdyaev's argument that the Church has denied the creativeness of the Spirit by its emphasis upon 'obedience' is very relevant here.

man in the structures of his historical existence. As Reinhold
Niebuhr says,[12] the view that all things have their source in
God must always be balanced by the view that all things have
their fulfilment in God: without the latter, the former becomes
a mere pantheistic acceptance of life as it is – which Camus and
others rightly condemn. We have already seen that fulfilment
has nothing to do with the laying down of dogmatic pre-emptions or of submission to a pre-ordained divine programme.
Nevertheless, we do not act blindly in meeting the secular
challenge, nor is our task merely the pragmatic one of trying
something to see if it works only to end up with Sisyphus at the
bottom of the mountain because absurdity always has the last
word. We act in a world in which Christ has already acted,
and we seek to align ourselves with him in the belief that his
way – the way of love – is the way things ultimately are and
that in him our work will not be in vain. The fact that our
achievement falls far short of his reminds us that we are still
'pestiferous' men and ought to keep us from the presumptuous-
ness of claiming absolute authority for our programmes or
finality for our insights.

In conclusion, it is interesting and indeed devastating to notice
the way in which the word 'theology' is being used today in
political contexts. To refer to a political doctrine as 'theology'
is to imply blind belief in and wholesale application of views
which are now irrelevant to the political realities of the time.
Nothing could reveal more clearly the secular opinion of what
Theology itself is and it is right that modern theologians should
repudiate it by their emphasis upon the disclosure of theological
truth within the concrete realities of our mundane existence.
But as I have tried to argue the truth that is in Jesus belongs to
the divine as well as to the human context and necessarily transcends and questions our secular structures. There is an inescapable sense in which Theology *is* a setting out of timeless, 'metaphysical' truth: that truth is, I believe, the content, the style,
the substance of the divine rebellion, initiated and endorsed
by God, actualized in the world by Christ, and made permanently available to all who align themselves with the way of

Christ through the Holy Spirit 'for the bane and enlightening of men'. To be a Christian is to have one's own tragic protest taken up into the Protest of Christ and to find that in him it meets a reality beyond our dreaming.

> Those who believe that they believe in God, but without any passion in their heart, without anguish of mind, without uncertainty, without doubt, without an element of despair even in their consolation, believe only in the God-Idea, not in God himself.[13]

Notes

1. A. Camus, *The Myth of Sisyphus*, Hamish Hamilton, London 1955 and Alfred A. Knopf, New York 1955.

2. A. Camus, *The Rebel*, Hamish Hamilton, London 1953 and Alfred A. Knopf, New York 1954.

3. A. Camus, *The Plague*, Hamish Hamilton, London 1948, Penguin Books, 1960 and Alfred A. Knopf, New York 1948. The page references are to the Penguin edition.

4. P. Thody, *Albert Camus 1913-1960*, Hamish Hamilton, London 1961 and The Macmillan Co., New York 1962.

5. A. Camus, *The Fall*, Hamish Hamilton, London 1957, Penguin Books 1963 and Alfred A. Knopf, New York 1957.

6. *The Rebel*, p. 27.

7. A. Camus, *The Outsider*, Hamish Hamilton, London 1946 and Penguin Books, 1961. American title, *The Stranger*, Alfred A. Knopf, New York 1946.

8. II Cor. 5.21 (RV).

9. P. van Buren, *The Secular Meaning of the Gospel*, SCM Press, London 1963, Penguin Books, 1968 and The Macmillan Co., New York 1963.

10. Harvey E. Cox, *The Secular City*, SCM Press, London 1965, Penguin Books, 1968 and The Macmillan Co., New York 1965. The page references are to the original edition.

11. P. Tillich, *Systematic Theology, Vol. II*, James Nisbet, Welwyn Garden City 1957, p. 74 and University of Chicago Press, 1951.

12. R. Niebuhr, *An Interpretation of Christian Ethics*, Harper & Row, New York 1935 and Living Age Books, 1956, p. 137.

13. Unamuno, *The Tragic Sense of Life*, Macmillan, London 1921 and Collins Fontana Books, 1962, p. 193.

6

The Self and the System

It falls to the lot of few writers to succeed in identifying a feature
of life with such precision that it is thereafter immediately recognizable whenever it occurs. Such a writer was Franz Kafka
whose work has given us the adjective 'kafkaesque'. Almost any
newspaper will give examples of kafkaesque situations. The
edition of *The Times* issued on June 28 1966 said that an an-
nouncement had been made in the House of Commons on the
previous day by the Secretary of State for Commonwealth
Affairs, to the effect that exploratory talks with Rhodesian officials were to continue. A member had asked if the House could
know what there was now left to explore. The Secretary of State
had replied: 'Obviously there is still something worth exploring,
otherwise the talks would not be continuing.'

That exchange could have come straight out of a novel by
Kafka. It is an example of the absurd effect of an excess of logic,
which is the method by which Kafka presents the nightmare
world of his heroes. His stories are rather like those dreams in
which one finds oneself in a situation which is at once perfectly
lucid and entirely senseless. The logic is an endless *a* implies *b*
implies *a* implies *b* which leaves unanswered the question why *a*
should be *a* at all. As Camus says,[1] it is all rather like the story
of the lunatic who was fishing in a bath: the psychiatrist, trying
out a clever form of treatment, asked 'Are they biting?', and
received the reply, 'Of course not, imbecile, can't you see it's only
a bath?' The world of Kafka, remarks Camus, is a world in
which men are condemned to fish in a bath knowing that nothing
will ever come out of it.

The interpretation of Kafka's symbolic stories is extremely
difficult, and there are almost as many theories about them as

there are commentators. Some of the more recent commentators feel that our understanding of Kafka was in some respects misdirected by his friend and biographer Max Brod, whose authority as one who knew Kafka intimately naturally gave considerable weight to his opinions about Kafka's work. But Brod's interpretation of *The Castle*, for example, understanding it as the human quest for divine grace and making the castle itself a symbol of God, has been treated with contempt by Erich Heller, who describes Brod's view as a comic escapade of literary criticism.[2] Yet Heller's own interpretation, which takes the castle to be a stronghold of Gnostic demons and sees a Manichean theology in the incident when K drinks some of Klamm's brandy, is hardly less comic. The fact is that Kafka's strange and complex work, with its involuted logic and nightmarish inconsequentiality, requires an Archimedean point outside itself if its 'meaning' is to be grasped, and everybody's Archimedean point is different. What can at least be said is that nothing quite like Kafka's work had appeared before and not much serious writing has been uninfluenced by it since.* Kafka is required reading for any who would know how European man understands himself in the twentieth century.

Kafka's most important books are *The Trial*[3] and *The Castle*.[4] In both of them we are presented with man seeking to justify his existence. Joseph K, the hero of *The Trial*, is a competent bank official who is visited one morning at his lodgings by the police and told that he is under arrest. He is not informed of the charge against him, and the police depart leaving him where he is. At first, Joseph K, who can think of no crime he has committed, decides to ignore this absurd threat and to continue his life as usual. But by degrees it comes to dominate all his thoughts. He believes in the existence and impartiality of the Law and that it will speedily vindicate his innocence. But how can he gain access to the Law? Only through the judicial apparatus – courts, advocates, magistrates, judges, and so on. Yet at

* Charles Moeller finds parallels to Kafka in the music of Mahler, especially *Das Lied von der Erde* and *Des Knaben Wunderhorn*. But perhaps such a piece as Stockhausen's *Gruppen* would be nearer the mark!

every level this apparatus proves useless. Not knowing what crime he has committed, Joseph K cannot hope to assemble a case for the defence and can rely only on obtaining 'influence' in the right quarter. Such influence it is the purpose of his advocate, engaged by Joseph K on his uncle's advice, to create, but since the advocate is a sick man who seems to spend all his time in bed, his services do not promise results – or rather, they *promise* results but never obtain any. Joseph K's own efforts are equally fruitless, and in the end he is taken by two buffoon-like but courteous characters to a disused quarry and stabbed to the heart. He dies, as he says, 'like a dog', having had no opportunity to clear himself of the unknown charge. 'It was as if he meant the shame of it to outlive him.'

The Castle resembles *The Trial* in that its hero – referred to throughout the book simply as 'K' – is also engaged in a personal quest. He is a Land Surveyor who has been summoned to a village to do some special work. Instructions will come for him from the castle which stands on a hill overlooking the village and by which the village affairs are supposedly run. But all attempts by K to elicit authorization and instruction from the castle fail. He has an interview with the village superintendent who tells him that the castle has no need of a Land Surveyor and that the summons K has received might have been due to a mix-up between two departments. K tries to get in touch with Klamm, the representative of the castle in the village, and makes love to Klamm's mistress, the barmaid at the inn where Klamm has a room, in the hope that she will lead him to him; but he has no success. The castle does, however, send K two assistants, so that at least his presence and purpose in the village seem to be recognized; but the assistants are mere buffoons whose behaviour so exasperates K that he drives them away. A message comes from Klamm, but it is a senseless message congratulating him on his good work when he has not even started and does not know what he is meant to do. And when at last K does get through to the administration, and stumbles accidentally on one of the castle secretaries, he is too weary to take advantage of the opportunity, and falls asleep. The book simply stops; it does not end. There is no reason why it should end, for K's quest is interminable and only death can conclude it.

2

Kafka wrote these two novels before 1918 but they were not published until the 1920s. In some respects they show a remarkable prevision of later political developments in Europe. The treatment of Joseph K reminds us of the visits of the Gestapo to people's homes and the arbitrary arrest of a member of a family. Again, K and Joseph K are like displaced persons, refugees without papers who have lost their fatherland and are unable to find acceptance in another but are condemned to wait endlessly in corridors in order to catch the eye of an official who may take up their case. And the judicial apparatus of *The Trial* and the administrative apparatus of *The Castle* put us in mind of those heartless bureaucratic and totalitarian systems by which our century has been and is afflicted. We cannot be reminded too often of the outrages committed in the names of security, solidarity, and progress. There are plenty of potential Gauleiters and commissars in every society, and a society which is foolish or weak enough to give them power is choosing its own damnation. Even at less extreme limits than these it is hard to avoid a feeling that the freedom and integrity of the individual are in our time under grave danger. As societies become more complex, so the administration of them becomes more remote from personal values. Perhaps no one is safe from the nocturnal rap on the door and imprisonment without trial : probably most of us have kafkaesque nightmares in which we find ourselves struggling vainly to state our case before some stone-faced official, knowing that we are condemned in advance and our lives are already forfeit. This is not merely a groundless neurosis but a recognition of what has happened and is now happening to a considerable number of people in this century and from which no one is entitled to think himself immune. The reality of such experience has been the subject of many books, notably of Koestler's political novels[5] and Orwell's *1984*, but perhaps Kafka was the first to identify it for us as a tendency of our time. His most fearsome story, *In the Penal Settlement*,[6] describes a machine called the Harrow which gradually cuts more and more deeply into its victim's flesh the crime of which he is accused – and which he himself does not know until he reads it in his own wounds. We have the distinction of living in an age in which Kafka's stories could be the sober truth. The Hungarian writer Georg Lukács, who was imprisoned in a weird castle in Rumania after the Hungarian rising of 1956, is said to have remarked, 'So Kafka was a realist after all!' Perhaps the greatest tribute was paid by the East German Minister of Culture after the occupation of Czechoslovakia by Russia and the other Warsaw Pact countries. He blamed Kafka for corrupting the Czechoslovak intellectuals, and said that their reverence for Kafka was a kind of 'spiritual rape' and had been 'the mental preparation for those events which have plunged our neighbour-nation into the deep crisis exploited by counter-revolution' (*The Times*, September 6 1968). The relevance of Kafka to the agonies of our time could hardly be more cogently demonstrated.

The apparatus of *The Trial* and *The Castle* is not only sinister; it is also inefficient and inept. Officials hunt through vast disordered piles of documents and fail to find the one they are looking for. Interminable forms are filled in only to be filed away and never read. Messengers are not sure which official they are supposed to serve. The office staffs work furiously but nothing ever seems to come of their work except a deluge of papers. In Orson Welles' film of *The Trial*, there was a vast cavernous building (it was actually a disused railway station in Paris) filled with row upon row of typists all pounding their machines and filling the air with an appalling noise – and yet neither Joseph K nor any of the hundreds of other clients could find the official they wanted or obtain any information about their cases. One feels that Kafka's fantastic bureaucracy has long ago forgotten the purpose of its labours and has become entirely absorbed in maintaining its own system. The officials work not for the public service but for each other, as though Parkinson's Law had been taken to its ultimate conclusion. The administration simply ministers to itself.

This picture of bureaucracy gradually strangling itself with its own red tape, as Heller puts it, is both comic and tragic. Anyone who has worked for the Public Service will recognize the truth behind the exaggeration. Kafka's picture is a parody, but in this matter as in so many others nature frequently imitates art. There is, however, little comicality in the system for the wretches who are trying to extract information or help from it. Part of the difficulty is that bureaucracy develops its own logic, its own internal consistency, which, because it can be understood only from the inside, seems senseless and derisory to the outside observer or client. We all have stories about dealings with organizations which, after vast effort and piles of correspondence, simply end where they started. And we have a sneaking feeling that the fault may be our own because we have failed to understand the system. This is the position of K and Joseph K in Kafka's two novels. They are wearied and exasperated by the endless frustrations caused by what seems to be the baffling chaos of the administration; and yet they also suspect that they are themselves at fault in their failure to grasp its logic. Perhaps they are adopting methods and applying criteria which simply do not fit the system with which they have to deal. They bombard the system with questions, they try to ingratiate themselves with influential officials, they express anger when nothing seems to be happening – in short they make thorough nuisances of themselves. Perhaps after all, as K at one point ironically thinks, it would have been better to proceed very quietly, not drawing attention to oneself but adopting an attitude of humility and patience in recognition of one's own ignorance and inexperience. K feels that he got off on the wrong foot from the start when, on the night of his arrival in the village, a telephone call was made about him to the castle, thus drawing the attention of the castle to himself and perhaps making the authorities angry. If he had first settled quietly in the village without disturbing the Central Bureau, he might have been successful. 'The authorities would have pursued the matter further, but calmly, in the ordinary course of business, unharassed by what they probably hated most, the impatience of a waiting client.'

3

We have so far pictured Kafka's apparatus as a parody of an all too human bureaucratic system which has lost sight of the purpose it is meant to serve and simply maintains its own enclosed existence. But this is only one layer of Kafka's meaning. No bureaucracy could so consistently disappoint reasonable expectation. We must therefore look for other meanings.

Perhaps it is best to begin at the beginning and ask why Kafka's heroes ever find themselves in their puzzling predicaments. We shall probably be right in thinking that K and Joseph K are meant to represent Everyman and are not merely freakish victims of particular circumstances. We notice that neither K nor Joseph K feels wholly innocent. Joseph K's landlady tells him not to worry about his supposed arrest. 'Above all you mustn't take it too much to heart,' she says, 'lots of things happen in this world . . . you are under arrest, certainly, but not as a thief is under arrest. If one's arrested as a thief, that's a bad business, but as for this arrest – it gives me the feeling of something very learned . . . it gives me the feeling of something abstract which I don't understand.' The landlady is expressing what is obviously the common-sense view about K's arrest: it is all so vague that it cannot be worth bothering about. Joseph K agrees with her. 'What you've just said is by no means stupid, Frau Graubach, at least I'm partly of the same opinion, except that I judge the whole thing still more severely and consider this assignation of guilt to be not only abstract but a pure figment.' Yet it is very soon apparent that Joseph K does not believe that the affair is 'a pure figment'. He is informed by telephone that on the following Sunday an inquiry into his case will be held, and he is told to present himself at a house in an outlying suburban street. K's reaction is an immediate decision to 'fight' the case. He appears at the inquiry in a bellicose mood and makes an aggressive speech complaining about the business of his arrest, the behaviour of the police, and the competence of the Examining Magistrate. This is hardly the common-sense attitude of a man who regards the case against him as a 'pure figment'. Most of us would say, as the landlady does, that mistakes can happen and the inquiry will quickly reveal the error and settle the matter. But not Joseph K. He protests too much and too violently so that his denial of guilt seems not genuine. The court itself gains this impression. 'I merely wanted to point out,' says the Examining Magistrate, as K is about to rush from the courtroom, 'that today you have flung away with your own hands all the advantages which an interrogation invariably confers on an accused man.'

But what is the crime of which Joseph K is guilty? I think we must assume it to be true that there is no specific charge against him, and yet at the same time he feels culpable. His crime is not a figment, but nor is it specific. Perhaps the landlady's word 'abstract' may be the clue we want. Joseph K's crime is the crime of existing – the crime not of doing, but of being. He is an exemplar of Kafka's own remark that 'the state in which we find ourselves is that of being sinners independently of a fault'.[7] And it is because of this inner disquiet, brought to the surface by the absurd 'arrest', that Joseph K gradually hands himself over to the accusing apparatus.

It is noteworthy that, apart from the first summons already mentioned, Joseph K does not receive any further word from his accusers. It is he who takes the initiative, engages an advocate, and seeks access to the persons concerned with his case. And in the end, he accepts his execution as inevitable: there is no expression of surprise or protest when the two mysterious men lead him away. It is true that he refuses to plunge the knife in his own breast when it is offered to him, but this is only because he is so worn out that he has not 'the remnant of strength necessary for the deed'. All he knows is that 'he has been condemned by a judge he has never seen in a high court to which he has never penetrated' (R. Pascal). He dies helplessly, 'like a dog'. There is no sympathiser, no good man to help him. But the point has been reached at which it is easier to accept condemnation than to continue the exhausting struggle against it.

4

'We are sinners,' said Kafka, 'independently of a fault.' What

we have in Kafka's heroes is the same sense of an unjustified
existence as we have noticed in those of Sartre. The difference
is that Sartre demands *self*-justification as the only possible exit
from absurdity, but Kafka knows that there can be no such
exit. As Heller says, the intellect may dream its dream of freedom
but the heart knows its terrible bondage.

What does it mean to describe guilt as 'existential'? How is it
that Kafka can say that we are sinners independently of a fault?
What kind of experience is being pointed out to us by Joseph K
in his frantic and fruitless efforts to prove his innocence?

Perhaps as good an example as any is the kind of feeling one
gets when one is accused of some kind of failure in one's job
or in any enterprise in which one is anxious to be successful.
It makes little difference whether or not the criticism is felt to
be just. One may seek to give the impression that one is unruffled
by it, but even the toughest character may lose some of his inner
assurance. The effect may be felt as a kind of cracking of one's
inner self – as though one were becoming fragmented, as though
the solidity of one's central being were breaking up. In extreme
form, it is the experience Dostoevsky indicates when he makes
Raskolnikov say, 'It wasn't the old woman I killed. It was myself.'[8] There is a questioning of the fundamental choice of the
self – not merely of what I have done, but of what I *am*. Human
beings are precariously poised in their central being: it takes
little to knock us over, to make us feel that we are no longer
capable of affirming our own personal reality. I believe that
Kafka is saying that we cannot make this affirmation of ourselves
without participation in an order of meaning, a set of values,
by which we feel ourselves to be supported. It is impossible to
attack a man's actions without at the same time attacking his
inner being – what he is to himself. What Kafka's heroes discover is that they cannot continue to live in a world of accusation
and rejection: there is a gradual corrosion of the soul, a loss of
integrity, which the individual is powerless to arrest, and in the
end he dies because he has rejected himself. Nearly all Kafka's
stories are concerned with this 'existential' guilt. The metamorphosis of Gregor[9] into an obscene insect leads to rejection by
his family, but Gregor has forestalled them. His existential guilt

has taken an outward form: it is as though the Psalmist's self-accusing cry, 'I am a worm and no man', had become literally true.

One form of what Kierkegaard called 'the sickness unto death' is the despair of not willing to be oneself.[10] The seeds of this despair are present in us all and they are fertilised by the accusation of others. It is as if the despair in us springs up to meet the accusation, as though it were merely waiting for the smallest pretext to assert its presence. And our courage to be ourselves ebbs away, and leaves us, like the small animal in Kafka's story *The Burrow*,[11] lying terrified, with our hands over our ears trying to shut out the hissing noise which spells destruction – only it cannot be shut out for it comes from within. The reason why political prisoners can be made to confess to crimes they have not committed is surely to be found here. Accusation uncovers the guilt which lies at the centre of a man's being – the guilt which is present in him independently of a fault – and his confession is not really of the crimes with which he is charged but of his central despair, his *self*-accusation. What normally saves us from self-rejection is our participation with other people in an affirming structure of love; we are able to accept ourselves through the acceptance of others. We have seen that this procedure is repudiated by Sartre because it is the way of the 'salaud' who has to appear in order to be, but we have also seen that there is reason to question the extreme individualism of Sartre. What we have in Kafka's novel *The Castle* is man's search for the justification of his existence through others – his attempt to become part of a system of values in which his own selfhood will be affirmed. For Kafka knows that such values cannot be generated out of a man's own despair. The self he attempts to assert is always a broken self which eludes and puzzles both the individual and other people. In spite of their confident attitudes, K and Joseph K are frightened men, trying, but without success, to recreate their broken selves through the Other. Their mistake lies in their wrong identification of this Other: they look for salvation to an apparatus and turn their backs on personal being. They lose love in an effort to attain law.

This may be the explanation of the enigmatic parable about

the Doorkeeper and the Law in *The Trial*. It is told to Joseph K
by the chaplain towards the end of the novel, and it concerns
a man who is seeking access to the Law. He comes to a doorway
through which the light of the Law shines but his way through
is barred by a Doorkeeper who tells him that he cannot enter yet.
So the man sits down to wait, and he waits there all his life. He
is never told why he may not enter, and this is the one question
which the numerous commentators on this piece of 'scripture'
do not answer. We have seen that Joseph K believes that the Law
lies somewhere beyond the fantastic maze of the judicial administration, and if only he can find his way through the apparatus
the Law will be there and his vindication will be assured. But
here in the parable is a man who has actually succeeded in
this – he has reached the very threshold of the Law beyond the
apparatus, and yet the Law is still as inaccessible to him as ever.
The existence of the Law is attested by the light which shines
through the doorway; it is a reality, and yet it is out of reach.
Why?

Perhaps part of the answer is simply that the Law cannot save.
The man who seeks legal vindication of his right to exist does
so in solitude: he becomes obsessed by his demand for justification and loses human comradeship. It is hard not to think
that Kafka has the Jewish Law in mind in this parable: the prophetic judgment on those who lay claim to a legal righteous-
ness divorced from humane feeling and social obligation may
lie behind the refusal of access. The man in the parable wonders
why no one else has come seeking the Law, and the Doorkeeper
tells him that this entrance is intended for him alone. It is his
entrance, yet he is not permitted to enter. He is excluded because he cannot be justified by himself: the way of justification,
which is the way to the presence of God, is the way of community, the way of compassion, the way of fellowship with my comrades and even with all the world. As Berdyaev says in *Spirit
and Reality*, 'the idea of personal salvation is a transcendent egoism, a projection of egoism upon eternal life. One cannot be
saved alone. Isolated salvation is impossible. One can be saved
only with one's neighbour, with other men, with the world.
Each one must take upon himself the sorrow and suffering of

the world and of men, and share in their destiny.'[12] Kafka's
parable tells us that the man whose mind is Pharisaic, the man
who abandons sinful humanity and claims a private rectitude,
cannot enter the Kingdom of Heaven.

Of course Kafka's heroes are not Pharisees, but they are
searching for an individual vindication which is pharisaical in
intent. The hero of *The Castle* has left his wife and children
and seems to spare no thought for them. In the village itself,
people point out to him that his desire to gain recognition by
the castle is causing him to act in an inhuman way towards
those who have offered him their friendship and even their love.
Are we meant to understand that K's desire for justification is
a selfish desire which is bound to fail precisely because it involves him in a misuse of other people? There is a strong suggestion that his dismissal of the assistants, useless as they are
in his own enterprise, is a heartless act on K's part, prompted by
the obsession of his quest. Again, K cannot deny Frieda's accusation that he has made love to her merely because she is
Klamm's mistress and may therefore be useful to him. It
looks as if K is trying to get himself into the position of being
able to trust in the castle that he is righteous and despise others.
His own state is very similar to that of Pepi, the chambermaid
who supplants Frieda in the taproom of the inn. Pepi, K tells
her, is like a child who 'tugs at the tablecloth, gaining nothing,
but only bringing all the splendid things down on the floor and
putting them out of its reach for ever'. Pepi is like this – but so
also is K. Their aspirations have been defeated by the selfish
violence with which they have pursued them.

5

Kafka's meanings are notoriously hard to pin down. They merge
into one another, the focus constantly shifts, no point of view
attains finality. It is a world in which every proposition is true
and every proposition has a contradictory opposite which is also
true, so that the truth of the one is always falsified by the truth
of the other and truth and falsity become identical. Sometimes
one is on the side of the hero in his genuinely human urge to

find values by which his selfhood will be affirmed; but at other times it is clear that the quest is futile because the apparatus on which it pins its hopes is obviously bogus and can minister only to final disillusion and despair. As Erich Heller says, the heroes of Kafka know two things at once: that there *is* no God and that there *must* be a God. And they are half aware that their quest is itself nullified by the object it seeks and that their failure is due to 'their own complicity with the forces which destroy them' (Moeller). In short, the apparatus continues to exist only because people continue to believe in it: scepticism would destroy it, but K and the credulous villagers seem to be incapable of scepticism. Only one person in the village has dared to defy the castle: she is a girl called Amalia who has refused a summons from one of the officials, Sortini. The result of Amalia's defiance is that she and her family are ostracized by the village and her father wears himself out in his efforts to obtain pardon from the castle. Amalia herself remains resolute, and the significant thing is that *nothing happens to her*. The power of the castle has been challenged and proved to be spurious. Yet no one in the village, not even K, has understood the import of Amalia's action – namely, that the power of the castle exists only in the minds of those who believe in it. Or perhaps K does half recognize this but prefers to cling to a bogus faith rather than to surrender to final despair.

Above all, Kafka's heroes are men who never experience grace. There may be an exception to this in Frieda's love for K, but otherwise the statement stands. To them the heavens are always brass: there is no unexpected mercy, no unlooked-for help, no good man to intervene on their behalf. They have to fight every inch of the way and do not even gain what they have struggled for. God, if he is not dead, is certainly silent, and no messenger from the kingdom of light ever gets through to these exiles. The apparatus, which is supposed to facilitate his journey, implacably bars his way.

'The question of the twentieth century,' says Camus, 'has gradually been specified: how to live without grace and without justice.'[13] The answer of Kafka to this question would seem to be that it is impossible to live without grace and without justice.

But is this all that Kafka has to say to us? Where does the error of Kafka's heroes lie? Is it in the quest itself or in the direction which the quest takes? I believe that the mistake is in the direction, not in the quest. I think Kafka implies that grace and justice *do* exist, but that twentieth-century man is looking for them in the wrong places and trying to find them by the wrong method. His rationality, his techniques, his boundless curiosity, his determination to know, to hold reality in his grasp – these abilities, which have served so well in the fields of production and organization, fail miserably when it comes to an understanding of and justification for existence itself. Erich Heller aptly quotes *All's Well that Ends Well*:

> They say miracles are past; and we have our philosophical persons, to make modern and familiar things supernatural and causeless. Hence it is that we make trifles of terrors, ensconcing ourselves into seeming knowledge, when we should submit ourselves to an unknown fear.

Heller's comment is, 'In Kafka we have the abdication of the philosophical persons.'[14] To use Kafka's own image in *The Great Wall of China*,[15] modern man is like a river which has overflowed its banks. He has pushed his inquiries too far, like a river which, forgetting its own proper limits, has lost its outline and shape and tries to ignore its destiny by forming little seas in the interior of the land. There is, says Kafka, a very wise maxim: 'Try with all your might to comprehend the decrees of the High Command, but only up to a certain point; then avoid further meditation.' There are two reasons for this restraint: one is that, if we knew the full extent of the labour required of the human race, we should become disheartened; the other is that we might come to think that our toil is useless, serving no intelligible purpose and supported by no enduring values. Modern man has, in fact, made both these discoveries. The Emperor has sent us a message from his death-bed, but the imperial messenger has been obstructed and the message has not been delivered. The present Emperor is equally unknown, and it is not far from the truth to draw the conclusion that 'in reality we have no Emperor'. That is, precisely, the conclusion which twentieth-century man *has* drawn: he has pushed his inquiries too far

and has established 'a fundamental defect' which undermines
'not only our consciences, but, what is far worse, our feet'. Thus
man finds himself in despair because he can discover no relation
between existence and truth. He is, as Nietzsche said, like a man
standing on very thin ice across which a thawing wind is blow-
ing:* the realities by which we have been supported in the past
have become too thin to bear our weight, and we are breaking
through into the watery abyss beneath. Our efforts to establish
a secure existence, our technical achievements, our address to
the secular challenge, our Great Wall of China – all this becomes disheartening if there is no eternity to affirm the con-
ception of an hour, no transcendental aim to nerve and direct
our labour, no awareness of a grace which breaks in on us from
a source beyond the pragmatic demands of the immediate task
and irradiates our vision.

Kafka's heroes, I have suggested, are looking for grace and
justice in the wrong places. It is also the case that they are using
the wrong method: their inquiries serve merely to put out of
reach what they are seeking to grasp. The method is that which
for convenience we may call *positivism*, whose symbol and instrument is the filing-system. The administration of the castle is
wholly dominated by files, and Kafka's description of the distri-
bution of files to the various officials at the start of the working
day is perhaps the most ludicrous scene in the book. An official
without a file is a helpless nonentity, and an official with fewer
files than his colleagues is a jealous child. The actual people to
whom the files refer are never mentioned: the administration
has become a closed system, and the physical presence of K, on
whose case there is presumably a file even if it is no more than
a scrap of paper, disturbs the officials and hampers their work.
K is not merely irrelevant, he is a nuisance. So far as the administration is concerned, he *is* his file. The official can cope with
anything systematized, but real people merely disturb his neatly
co-ordinated organization. The picture is the positivist picture of

* 'The ice which still carries has become very thin: the thawing wind
blows; we ourselves, the homeless ones, are an agency that breaks the
ice, and the other too thin "realities" . . .' *The Joyful Wisdom*, p. 343, tr.
Common.

a world totally enclosed within itself in which every fact is cross-referenced with every other fact and nothing has any reality of its own.

Yet surely K is himself a victim of this positivistic parody. He continues to believe that the justification of his own existence is to be found in this absurd apparatus; somewhere there is a file in which he is defined and an official responsible for it. K entirely fails to see that, even if such a file does exist, it will refer, not to him, but only to other files kept by other officials which will ultimately refer back to the original and leave him exactly where he started. Here, I believe, we have *the impossibility of the human attempt to wrest the meaning of existence out of the secular context*, to find ultimacy in the mundane, to live in a world which is 'sealed off against any transcendental intrusion' (Heller). The castle represents the absurdity of the positivist claim to incorporate the whole of reality into phenomena and to capture human life in sociological and psychological classifications. What positivism fails to do is to give a man any insight into his own selfhood or to provide him with any reason for affirming his central being against the depersonalizing forces of secular systems and the burden of his own past.

The philosophical persons who, as Erich Heller says, have abdicated in Kafka, are those who would reduce the mystery and terror of human existence to something which can be handled by bureaucrats. Since this reduction is actually impossible, the pretence of its achievement can be claimed only by depriving the transcendental realm of its reality, by proclaiming the Emperor's death and blocking the path of his messenger, thus leaving us free to complete our filing-system and to offer it as the repository of all knowledge. By this procedure, modern man has shut out the marvellous and come near to losing his soul. He has pushed his empirical inquiries beyond the levels at which they yield knowledge and has drawn the conclusion that a transcendental order does not exist because it cannot be docketed. The result is a world which lies under a curse, conscious of its own damnation, in which the Great Wall of China excludes the messengers of light but totally fails to keep out the demons. When man looks for security instead of salvation, he loses both.

Kafka has 'uncovered the hidden estrangement of everyday life' (Anders), and has revealed to us a condition in which, as Heller says, 'systems have attained their final stranglehold and their final futility'.

6

Commentators on Kafka's work can be divided into those who consider its final word to be despair, and those who, beyond the despair, find a place for hope. Among the latter, Roy Pascal notices in *The Castle* a gradual softening of K's attitude towards the villagers – 'a breaking through his painful egocentricity to recognize the reality of other persons'.[16] Charles Moeller thinks that Kafka witnesses to 'the choice of a hope again become humble which prefers to accuse itself rather than put in question the world and curse the universe'.[17] Erich Heller claims that the power to experience and create Kafka's world must have its source *outside* that world: 'Only a mind keeping alive in at least one of its recesses the memory of a place where the soul is truly at home is able to contemplate with such creative vigour the struggles of a soul lost in a hostile land.'[18] Kafka's friend Max Brod, to whom we owe the rescue of Kafka's books from the author's instruction that they were to be burnt, has said that *The Castle* was meant to end on a note of vindication and hope. When K, worn out by his struggle, is on his death-bed, word was to come from the castle that the authorities were to permit him to live and work in the village. But I think it is easier to see this statement as the final irony of Kafka's work rather than as the satisfaction which Brod claims it to be: salvation has, after all, come too late, and we are simply reminded of the heartless futility of the whole system. It has a parallel in the closing scene of *The Trial*, when Joseph K, as his eyes are dimming in death, sees a person who may be his rescuer leaning out towards him through an open window. This is surely the last outrage of the demonic powers which have made sport of Kafka's heroes and compelled them to live a life of deferred hope which makes the heart sick. I cannot think that Kafka meant it as a happy ending, and those who think that the last word is despair are,

I am convinced, correctly defining Kafka's own intention.

But this is not to say that those who see hopeful implications beyond the despair are wrong. Kafka has shown that modern man's way of salvation leads not to heaven but to hell: yet there remains the possibility that there is another way – a way by which man may break out of the circular logic of the apparatus and attain that realm of the spirit in which his being can be made whole. We can, I think, draw some conclusions from Kafka's work.

Kafka's heroes are men who cannot find justification within themselves: they search endlessly and obsessionally for exterior values by which their existence may be supported. In this respect, they are very different from the heroes of Sartre and Camus, who have abandoned the hope of finding meanings outside the self and have decided to create their own. Men like Roquentin and Rieux have, as it were, passed through the illusory hopes of K and Joseph K and have come to the conclusion that there is no justification of human existence or human action in exterior systems. Those who wait in the hope of some cosmic disclosure which will establish their identity are thereby disqualified from their part in the human rebellion; so long as they look for some distant salvation they are unable to address themselves to the problems which demand their total attention here and now. Hope is thus the enemy of action because it takes our minds off the immediate context of our life and divides truth from actuality. But Kafka's heroes have not perceived this. They belong, as it were, to the age of faith, to the centuries in which men bowed down in humility before the universe and failed to grasp their autonomy. The astonishing thing is that the repeated disappointments of K and Joseph K do not extinguish hope. There is no grace for them but they continue to expect it because existence is intolerable if one cannot lock oneself on to a reality which transcends one's own selfhood. The self can be affirmed only within an affirming structure of values, and self-acceptance is difficult without acceptance by the Other. Kafka's heroes are separated from the Other and are therefore in a condition of inescapable self-doubt similar to the unsupported 'nothingness' of a Roquentin. But neither K nor Joseph K can take Roquentin's step of projecting himself out of nothingness; for them there is no self-salvation.

Or rather it would be more accurate to say that there is no salvation *within* the self, for Kafka's heroes certainly desire salvation *of* the self and all their efforts are directed towards this egocentric end. Their error is to suppose that they can be saved in solitude: other people are merely accessories to the scheme, to be discarded when they cease to be useful. Our second conclusion is that Kafka's heroes are profoundly mistaken in their identification of the Other by which they believe their self-hood will be affirmed: it is the impersonal Other of manipulators and mandarins whose claim to be the administrative staff of the kingdom of ends is entirely bogus. It is true that man cannot affirm himself without commitment to a reality by which his self-affirmation will be endorsed and transcended; but he can and does make terrible mistakes about the nature of that reality. However we may interpret Kafka's symbolic apparatus, there can be no doubt that it is an instrument of damnation. Man cannot be saved by systems which compel him to abandon his comrades. The political exile certainly desires a new fatherland, acceptance of his citizenship by a State in which he hopes to start his life again, official 'recognition', and so on. But none of this recognition is worth much if it does not make possible the discovery of new comrades.

> What do you think refugees do from morning to night? They spend most of their time telling one another the story of their lives. The stories are anything but amusing, but they tell them to one another, really, in an effort to make themselves understood. As long as there remains a determination to understand and to share one's understanding with others, perhaps we need not altogether despair.[19]

To understand others and to be understood by them – that is the essential human hope which enables us to continue to exist. But Kafka's heroes, in their very efforts to gain a place in the 'filing system', have deprived themselves of the possibility of comradeship and have reduced their selfhood to meaninglessness. Kafka has shown how human beings go wrong in their quest for that justification of their existence without which they cannot live. He has set up warning signs indicating a dead end. But he has not said that every way is a dead end. His warnings may help us to re-route our quest along the way which leads to truth and life. And that is the hope that is born in a man out of Kafka's despair. We have eaten of the tree of knowledge: now we must eat of the tree of life.

Notes

1. Camus, *Le Mythe de Sisyphe*, Appendix entitled *L'espoir et l'absurde dans l'oeuvre de Franz Kafka*.

2. E. Heller, *The Disinherited Mind*, Bowes and Bowes, Cambridge 1952 and Penguin Books, 1961.

3. F. Kafka, *The Trial*, tr. Willa and Edwin Muir, Secker and Warburg, London 1945 and Penguin Books, 1953.

4. F. Kafka, *The Castle*, tr. Willa and Edwin Muir, Secker and Warburg, London 1930, Penguin Books, 1957 and Alfred A. Knopf, New York 1930.

5. E.g. *Darkness at Noon*, Jonathan Cape, London 1940, Penguin Books and the Macmillan Co., New York 1941.

6. F. Kafka, *In the Penal Settlement*, in *Metamorphosis and Other Stories*, Secker and Warburg, London 1933 and Penguin Books, 1961.

7. Quoted by Moeller, *op. cit.*, Tome III, p. 229.

8. F. Dostoevsky, *Crime and Punishment*.

9. F. Kafka, *Metamorphosis*.

10. S. Kierkegaard, *The Sickness unto Death*, Princeton University Press, 1941 and Anchor Books 1954.

11. F. Kafka, *The Burrow*, in *Metamorphosis etc*.

12. N. Berdyaev, *Esprit et Réalité*, Aubier, Paris 1943, p. 208.

13. A. Camus, *The Rebel*, p. 195.

14. Heller, *op. cit.*, p. 180.

15. F. Kafka, *The Great Wall of China*, in *Metamorphosis etc*.

16. R. Pascal, *The German Novel*, Methuen & Co., London 1965.

17. Moeller, *op. cit.*, Tome III, p. 304.

18. Heller, *op. cit.*, p. 201.

19. Ignazio Silone, 'The Choice of Comrades' in *Encounter* December 1954.

7

Lovers and Libertines

In Orwell's police state of *1984*,[1] love between the sexes is forbidden. The reason for this is that love operates in the area of personal freedom where it is impossible for the State to have control. As love cannot be controlled, it must be prohibited.

The linking of love with freedom is common, especially in the European romantic tradition where love is often presented as a refuge from the harsh demands of work and duty. 'Love,' as Carmen tells us, 'is a rebellious bird,' and we all know what happened to Don José's sense of military duty when it came into collision with 'l'amour'.[2] While it is clear that such subversive possibilities would have to be eliminated from the way of life presided over by Big Brother, yet even within far less rigidly organized systems love can be rather a nuisance to the planners and authorities. Indeed it can almost be said that romantic love flourishes most when the social and economic pressures against it are greatest – a state of affairs which disapproving fathers and guardians have frequently found themselves compelled to acknowledge. And the romantic writer bids us applaud when his 'Rosina', for the sake of love, deceives and outwits her legal guardian who has invoked his authority against her amorous schemes. The rebellious bird must break free from the net cast by the upholders of the official *mores*, even though, in the end, the happy pair themselves may achieve a relationship hardly distinguishable in its conventionality from that of their elders.

There are, of course, exceptions to the rule of reversion to conventional attitudes. Those for whom love is above all a liberation from the tedium of life do not take kindly to a permanent relationship which all too soon ceases to be liberation and lapses into boredom. One may instance the faithlessness of a Manon Lescaut or of Carmen herself, which seems to be due, not to immoderate sexual desire, but to the conviction that love cannot thrive in domesticated captivity. H. G. Schenk[3] quotes Shelley's declaration that the system of marriage is hostile to human happiness: 'Love is free: to promise for ever to love the same woman is not less absurd than to promise to believe the same creed,' and Schenk goes on to point out that this view led Shelley into 'an inextricable tangle of emotions'.

It is not surprising that the Romantic mind should have been strongly attracted to the chief exponent of this doctrine, Don Juan, whose remarkable schedule of conquests is listed in Leporello's famous Catalogue aria.[4]

It is precise and formidable. Six hundred and forty in Italy, two hundred and thirty-one in Germany, a hundred in France, ninety-one in Turkey, and in Spain, his home ground, a thousand and three. One feels some surprise that Don Giovanni did not count English ladies worthy of his attentions, but his score with the perhaps more compliant ladies of Europe is an impressive one. The catalogue is read out to Donna Elvira who is herself one of the thousand and three betrayed ladies of Spain, and it is Don Giovanni himself who instructs Leporello to make these astonishing disclosures. 'What, do I tell her everything?' asks Leporello incredulously. 'Yes, everything,' replies the Don, but he prudently withdraws from the scene before the catalogue is read. Mozart adds his own musical comments to da Ponte's words: the orchestra chuckles sardonically throughout Leporello's revelations, with the single exception of the two lines about Giovanni's preference for young innocents, where the bassoon gives to the music, for a brief moment, a dark, sad quality. Already there is a hint that we cannot accept Giovanni's own estimate of himself, and this short passage, occurring as it does in the middle of the libertine's philosophy, seems more telling than the obvious tragedy of the Commendatore's death at the very beginning of the opera.

Women, the Don tells Leporello, are as necessary to him as the bread he eats and the air he breathes. To the manservant's not unreasonable question, Why so many? he replies to the effect that exclusive devotion to one would be cruel to all the rest. Giovanni sees himself as a magnanimous man: his love-making gives the ladies pleasure, so obviously he ought to spread this happiness as widely as possible, even to the old and ugly. He is a fully committed utilitarian and has a strong disapprobation of those who would set limits to happiness. He believes in his creed sufficiently to die for it, and there is sublimity in his reiterated 'No' to the statue's demand for repentance. And when Hell receives him, the world is a sadder and certainly a duller place: the Don Ottavios, faithful, righteous, and alas boring, have taken possession.

2

It is perhaps seldom that the libertine's abilities match the claims of his philosophy, but Don Giovanni must be counted the exception. He is the seductive charmer par excellence, able to reach the womanhood of every woman and make her feel ennobled. We must not allow ourselves to be misled by the fact that, as Ernest Newman says, the majority of those who play Don Giovanni on the stage 'put us in mind only of a good-looking barber's apprentice with a respectable score at purely local targets'.[5] This merely proves what an exacting vocation it is. Giovanni possesses civilized elegance in the highest degree; his way with ladies is to charm them into surrender, to arouse their aesthetic as well as their sexual feelings. His accomplishments are those of Castiglione's courtier.

The European Romantic tradition, in some of its nineteenth-century manifestations, cannot believe that the world and the flesh will provide all that is necessary for salvation or that there are human beings who are content with earth and do not desire a spiritualized heaven. That is why some Romantic critics mis-interpret Don Giovanni and seek to cast him in their own romantic mould. Here, for example, is the comment of E. T. A. Hoffmann.

Through the trickery of the arch-fiend, the thought comes into Don Juan's mind that through love, through the enjoyment of women, there could be fulfilled on earth what dwells in our hearts merely as a promise of heaven, and is that very infinite longing which puts us into immediate rapport with the supernatural.

Restlessly fleeing from a beautiful woman to a more beautiful one; enjoying their charms with the most burning ardour, to the point of surfeit, to the point of destructive intoxication; always believing he had been deceived in his choice; always hoping to find the ideal of eventual satisfaction – Juan was finally bound to find all earthly life insipid and flat; and while he despised man in general he rebelled against the manifestation which, valued by him as the finest thing in life, had so bitterly deceived him.[6]

This description admirably fits the hero of Hoffmann's own 'Tales', who, in the opera version, is disillusioned successively by a mechanical doll, a singer, and a courtesan, and is left with nothing but drink and his poetic muse. But there is no hint of it in the da Ponte-Mozart opera. Don Giovanni is, precisely, *not* a romantic of this kind: he does not invest the love of women with a supernatural hope which it cannot support. He neither hopes nor despairs – he simply enjoys. The romantic picture of a tortured soul striving through the flesh to transcend its isolation yet ever sinking more and more deeply into frustration and despair – this picture is, I believe, false. For Giovanni, there is no division between flesh and spirit. For some forms of Romanticism, however, flesh is the ladder by which the heavenward ascent is made only to be kicked away because salvation is of the spirit and flesh has no part in it. 'Live?' says Axel to Sara in Villiers de l'Isle-Adam's prose-poem, 'our servants will do that for us.' After a night at the very summit of love, the future is exhausted and the earth has become 'a drop of frozen mud' offering only disillusion.[7] But for Don Giovanni there is no disillusionment in love because nothing more is desired. Moreover, love is always innocent – it belongs to the prelapsarian paradise which man and woman inhabited before they became conscious of the stone-eyed glare of morality. The question is not one of gaining a spiritual paradise *through* love: love is *itself* paradise, and its innocence is affirmed in the Giovanni-Zerlina duet:

> Andiam, mio bene, andiam,
> Le pene a ristorar
> D'un innocente amor!

Kierkegaard did not make the Romantic mistake of understanding Don Juan as the quest of the human soul for spiritual salvation. He is careful to point out that Don Juan is 'flesh incarnate, or the inspiration of the flesh by the spirit of the flesh'. In the kingdom of the sensuous, he goes on, 'language has no place, nor sober-minded thought, nor the toilsome business of reflection. There sound only the voice of elemental passion, the play of appetites, the wild shouts of intoxication; it exists solely for pleasure in eternal tumult. The first-born of this kingdom is Don Juan . . . Not until reflection enters does it appear as the kingdom of sin, but by that time Don Juan is slain, the music is silent.'[8]

The trouble is, of course – and this is a point which Kierkegaard seems to overlook – that this 'innocent' love has to be attained, not only by serenades, compliments and deceits, but also by violence – if not against women, certainly against their protectors and legitimate partners. For the world *has* fallen, morality *is* outraged, and Juan's paradise can be regained only by drawing a sword against the fathers, husbands and fiancés who guard the way to the tree of life. Unfortunately for the Don, the forces of morality are also supernatural, and his career therefore comes to a spectacular end. And on the whole, in spite of our celebration of the 'sensuous', we feel that his fate is not undeserved: seduction of the innocent and dispatch of the old may be capable of being brought to zero significance by the utilitarian calculus, but we rightly suspect a calculation which comes out so heavily in favour of the calculator. The ladies themselves may not necessarily agree with the Don's estimate of their happiness, and may well come to the conclusion that 'la libertà' is too short-lived to be worth the price of virtue. Only it seems a pity that the order of things has arranged that virtue shall be dull.

Yet in spite of our reservations Don Juan may still have instruction for us. No doubt it is the freedom to assert ardent feeling against the inhibiting effects of convention, a recovery of primal desire in a world which has set too high a value on order and control, a restoration of natural delight in the flesh in protest against an intellectualized, self-conscious sexual culture. It may be that the moralization of feeling has robbed us of this spontaneous delight and that Don Juan's philosophy asserts a necessary corrective. We half think that the Don Juans are lucky to be untroubled by conscientious scruples, even though we may suspect ourselves of being unequal to their exhausting vocations.

Since Don Juan was a Spanish nobleman, it is of special interest to read an assessment of him by a Spanish philosopher. Ortega y Gasset sees Don Juan as a symbol of vitality and spontaneity, and contrasts him with the 'Socratic' ideal of rationality and systematized knowledge. 'The man of the present day,' says Ortega, 'does not deny reason, but rejects and ridicules its pretensions to absolute sovereignty'; and he goes on, 'Don Juan revolts against morality because morality had previously risen in rebellion against life. Only when a system of ethics is current which affirms plenary vitality as its first rule, will Don Juan agree to submit.'[9]

If Ortega is right about 'the man of the present day', we should expect to find a frequent appearance of the Don Juan figure in modern literature, and a strong emphasis on feeling and 'vitality'. One such figure is the hero of Thomas Mann's novel, Felix Krull,[10] though Felix engages in a slightly less immoderate pursuit of women than Don Juan and has time to admire other features of life. Felix is, no doubt, more dandified than the Don: the latter was a good swordsman and something of an expert in unarmed combat. But there is the same zest, the same infectious high spirits, the same attractiveness, at once civilized and animal, and the same generosity. Felix delights in physical beauty – especially, it must be said, in his own, which is striking enough to make his artistic godfather liken him to the god Hermes – and the whole novel breathes an air of spontaneous delight in all that is natural. Felix accounts himself one of those fortunate persons 'in whose cradle some good fairy has placed the gift of responding to pleasure, a perpetual responsiveness in even the most unlikely circumstances', and although he has to admit that this sensitiveness also makes him vulnerable to pain, yet he is convinced that all else is outweighed by the increase of joy. To use a phrase of Georg Lukács, Felix is a man who celebrates 'the self-enjoyment of personality'.

Unlike Don Giovanni, Felix is not nobly born, but this fact is clearly a mere oversight on the part of Nature which is properly adjusted when he is given the opportunity to impersonate a wealthy marquis. That Nature should lavish splendid personal gifts on a man and then deny him the opportunity of enjoying them and sharing them with others, would be an intolerable injustice by which Nature herself would be impoverished. In Felix's world, there is a complete identity of the actual with the true, of the flesh with the spirit. It is the lovelessness of man that drives a wedge between them; it is man who, by his ugliness and envy, rends the fabric of Nature. Only in this split world is Felix an impostor and a cheat: in the paradisal world, the world in which flesh is conformed to spirit and spirit to flesh, he is a god.

It was in his old age that Thomas Mann gave us his final though still unfinished version of Felix Krull, this epitome of youthful elegance and life-affirming zest. The world is no longer a sanatorium occupied by neurotic intellectuals who have lost the faculty of spontaneous joy, but a multitudinous paradise full of deep harmonies and endless possibilities of pleasure. It is a world grown young again, and the old as well as the young share in its renewal. We are reminded of those two master-pieces of maturity, *The Tempest* and Verdi's *Falstaff*, and we are grateful that Mann's last word to us is one of gaiety of spirit and delight in the flesh.

3

Felix Krull is a genuine though non-violent Don Juan, whose delight in the natural order extends even to prehistoric animals. But it must be said that most other modern versions of the Don Juan myth represent on the whole a sad distortion of a splendid theme. Juan's civilized elegance has gone, and we are left with crudities and perversions which separate flesh from spirit and remind us of those forms of Gnosticism which denied the effect of bodily acts upon the soul and claimed a kingly freedom for their adherents which set them above the law. But as Clement of Alexandria remarked, the upholders of this view act not like

kings but like cringing slaves. Don Giovanni is no slave and
he is not afraid; neither is he one of those for whom the fleshly
act is all, having nothing to do with the soul's joy in good man-
ners and personal address. It is quite impossible to imagine him
seducing a noble lady in a gardener's shed. But in modern fiction
Don Juan has been metamorphosed into a gamekeeper or a
secret agent who fundamentally despises woman and uses her in
a way appropriate to the vulgarity of his own nature. The civilized delight has gone, and love has become a squalid exercise in
sensation.

Parallel to this devaluation of Don Juanism there is a devaluation of woman herself. Simone de Beauvoir has pointed
to the curious contradictions in the male estimate of woman.
Woman is always the 'other', whose mystery both fascinates
and repels. Sometimes, she is 'the eternal feminine' whose beauty
and wisdom can lead man out of his mundane preoccupations
with work and duty to the realm of spirit where all is fulfilment
and peace; at other times, she is the Circe who transforms man
into a beast, robs him of his will-power, and enslaves him to the
desires of the flesh : 'the perverse sorceress arrays passion against
duty . . . she detains the traveller far from home, she pours for
him the drink of forgetfulness'.[11] There are, however, some
heroes of modern fiction who have succeeded in avoiding both
these alternatives. They have eliminated woman's spiritual claims
and reduced her to flesh; but they have also moderated the
tyranny of flesh by turning sex into a secondary, take-it-or-leave-
it occupation. The hero of *The Outsider* thinks it would be quite
a good idea to arouse a girl's sexual feelings and then kick her
out of bed; de Montherland's bull-fighter proves his superiority
by refusing the reward offered by the girl who has dared him
to fight a particularly dangerous animal; Joe Lampton has only
a few scruples in rejecting the woman who pleases his flesh in
favour of the one who advances his career. The male estimate
of woman has seldom been lower than it is in some modern
fiction. No longer a Beatrice, she is not even a Circe. She is not
woman either, but an impoverished male fantasy.

As an example of the ruin into which the *romantic* tradition
has fallen, we may instance Golding's treatment of Sammy

Mountjoy's girl in *Free Fall*.[12] Her name is – significantly –
Beatrice, and Sammy seeks in her the mysterious beauty by
which a woman may sanctify a man's deepest longings and raise
him with her to heaven. But Sammy's Beatrice is very different
from Dante's. She is an ordinary, conventional, inarticulate girl,
wholly incapable of bearing the weight of her lover's idealization. Her response is timid and her conversation is banal: she
is a girl whose thoughts centre on domestic respectability in a
suburban house, and the spiritual hunger and physical ardour
of Sammy gradually turn to silence and despair. 'What had been
love on my part, passionate and reverent, what was to be a
triumphal sharing, a fusion, the penetration of a secret, raising
of my life to the enigmatic and holy level of hers, became a
desperately shoddy and cruel attempt to force a response from
her somehow. Step by step we descended the path of sexual exploitation until the projected sharing had become an infliction.'
Bored and ashamed, Sammy at last leaves his Beatrice. Near the
end of the novel, he sees her again. She has become an incurable
idiot in the care of a sanatorium, and when Sammy speaks to
her she urinates on the floor and over his shoes. Golding has
written the epitaph to Goethe's Eternal Womanhood which
leads us on high:[13] the romantic dream ends in idiocy, inconti-
nence, and the corruption of the flesh. 'Woman,' says Simone de
Beauvoir, 'is doomed to immanence'; but Golding has gone
further and doomed her to triviality.

It is not easy to understand what Golding means by the
Sammy-Beatrice relationship. Does he mean that the romantic
ideal is nonsense; that woman, so far from leading man heavenward, in fact destroys his idealism by her own spiritual inadequacy? Or does he mean that Sammy's feeling for Beatrice is
wholly self-centred, an effect of his 'fallenness', which makes his
relationship with her evil and destructive? Or does he mean
that any attempt to reach the being of another person must fail
because selfhood is defective and we are obliged in the end to
settle for a superficial relatedness in which the ontological questions – Who are you? What are you? What is it like to be you? –
are no longer asked?

It seems doubtful whether any clear answer to these alternatives can be derived from the novel: the complexity of Golding's work precludes clear answers. But it looks as if he is trying to establish 'a fundamental defect' in man's being which makes intersubjectivity impossible and must therefore lead to the collapse of romanticism. There is no such thing as 'Eternal Womanhood'; there are only finite human beings whose centredness is not in themselves but in the shifting, impermanent context of their lives. When the context is shattered, as that of Beatrice is by Sammy's desertion, nothing is left but the emptiness of idiocy.

4

We may think that the failure of Sammy and Beatrice is due, not to some general ontological defect, but to the mere fact that they are both unformed adolescents who have not yet had time to fill their subjectivity. But there are examples of similar failure in maturity as well as adolescence. Malcolm Lowry's novel *Under the Volcano*[14] portrays a couple in middle life whose feeling for each other is just as incommunicable as is that of Sammy for Beatrice. The novel is set in Mexico, and the central characters are the British Consul and his wife Yvonne. When the novel begins, the Consul is alone, his wife having left him some time before. He has written passionate, longing letters to her which he has never posted. He is an alcoholic. One day, suddenly and unexpectedly, his wife returns, and both of them hope to recreate the intensely happy relationship they knew in the early years of their marriage.

But each finds it impossible to touch the other's central being. Malcolm Lowry sets the banal, senseless events of the present in a richly elaborate context of the past and the future. The past is remembered by the Consul and his wife, but it is remembered individually and separately so that there is no common content to draw them together. They dream of a new life in the future, but there is no attainment of mutuality in the present. Life is lived in a kind of no-man's-land of torturing failure to communicate. There was value in the past and there are dreams of the future, but in the present there is nothing. Here are a man and a woman, both of high intelligence and rich imagination, both aware of the vast hinterland of memory and desire, yet for whom there is no correlation between inward longing and present actuality. Flesh and spirit are sundered, and the present is only an endless transition from the past to the future, an arbitrary succession of trivial events in which dreams and alcohol have become almost total substitutes for mutuality. At the end of the novel, both Yvonne and the Consul are killed. The last words are, 'Somebody threw a dead dog after him down the ravine.' Like Joseph K in *The Trial*, the Consul has died 'like a dog' because he has rejected himself and life has become worthless and intolerable.

In this subtle, complex tale, Malcolm Lowry has focused our attention on the baffling failure of the individual to break out of his isolation and to be 'present' for his beloved in the *now* of existence. Behaviour fails to communicate being; conversation and shared pleasures have no sacramental depth but serve rather to intensify the sense of forsakenness. The Consul is torn by an interior conflict between his desire that Yvonne should liberate him from his alcoholic solitude, and his resentment against her penetration of that solitude which, in another part of his being, he cherishes. Does woman liberate or does she enslave? Does the fire of love purify or does it destroy? Is the volcano a heavenward-aspiring mountain, or is it a funnel of hell? Stretched on the rack of these contraries, the Consul can be sure neither of Yvonne nor of himself. The Romantic dream has turned into a nightmare.

5

The radical questioning of Golding and Lowry has taken us far from the unreflecting zest of Don Juanism and from the lofty ideal of Romanticism. Of course it is far from exceptional for the novelist to present the married state as a condition of life characterized by conventionality and boredom and to contrast it with the grand passion of romantic love or the fleshly raptures of promiscuity. Golding and Lowry have shown how difficult and yet how necessary it is that a relationship should strike deeper roots than those of the romantic dream, but it must be admitted that the connubial virtues of loyalty, responsibility and mutual understanding do not lend themselves to exciting fictional treatment. We may instance the unendurable existence of the student-hero's wife in *The Ginger Man*,[15] who is condemned to a squalid, servile routine in the home while her husband takes up an entertaining career compounded of women, drink, and buffoonery. One looks almost in vain for any sign from the author of sympathy for the unfortunate wife he has created. He even imposes on her the (literally) crowning indignity of a lavatory which from time to time discharges its contents into the living-room below. In fairness it must be said that the hero does make a few feeble attempts to sustain his wife; but his poetic soul feels imprisoned in the confines of domesticity, and it is not long before libertinage becomes his preferred option. The theme is, of course, a familiar one; and the presupposition is that marriage dulls the creative spirit by its prosaic claims upon duty, work and self-denial. The connubial virtues are not compatible with byronic talents, and as Romanticism has taught us that self-realization is all, it is the former that become expendable.

Simone de Beauvoir flatly asserts that 'adultery . . . is indeed the form that love will assume so long as the institution of marriage lasts'.[16] While regarding this state of affairs as inevitable so far as the man is concerned, she demands a like freedom for the woman and elimination of the disparity between society's attitudes to the two cases. We notice that the lady novelist perhaps tends to endow her female characters with rather more sexual initiative than that permitted by male writers, and takes pleasure in undermining the male assumption of superiority. In Brigid Brophy's version of the Don Giovanni story, *The Snow Ball*, it is Donna Anna who refuses to allow the Don more than a single night of pleasure and turns him out of her house the next morning.[17] Iris Murdoch, in *A Severed Head*,[18] seems to enjoy describing the laughable astonishment of Martin Lynch-Gibbon when his wife Antonia announces that she loves another and wants a divorce. Lynch-Gibbon, who is himself unfaithful and considers marriage to be 'solemn but not uniquely sacred', cannot at first believe that his wife is serious. His struggle to be rational and modern in his attitude towards his wife and her lover while feeling a powerful primitive impulse to express his true feelings with violence, is highly comic. Although a man's wife may dwell merely in the suburbs of his affections, he takes it for granted that he dwells at the centre of hers, and great is his surprise and grievance when he discovers that the truth is otherwise.

Most modern novelists seem to share the view of Simone de Beauvoir that love never survives the conventionalizing effect of marriage. Love is presented either in terms of the varied but superficial excitements of a vulgarized Don Juanism, or as a means of making some sort of protest. The married state is seen as part of the *taedium vitae* which oppresses the 'organization man', who feels that he is a prisoner in the given social order. 'Love' then becomes a temporary exit from a predictable, banal existence rather than an all-consuming passion, and it not infrequently takes the form of crude sexual exploitation. The varieties of treatment of this theme are considerable, but there seems to be one safe generalization: the married man or woman in modern fiction seems incapable of achieving a mature relationship within the married state and easily reverts to adolescent and romantic attitudes.

How far this fictional account reflects an actual state of affairs is hard to determine. We have already noticed that a happy, conventional relationship provides poor material for the writer – but without therefore ceasing to exist. Nevertheless, the problems surrounding the man-woman conjunction do seem to be particularly acute in our time. No doubt marriage has always had its difficulties, but today they seem to have become more intense, perhaps because our hopes of happiness are pitched higher. We are feeling the effects, both good and bad, of European Romanticism. For centuries marriage had been understood as a 'state' into which people entered – a kind of paradigm having an objective existence as a social, legal, and even divine structure. The married state was not one which had to be created: it was already given, laid down in advance, demanding of those who entered it a simple conformity to its traditional *mores*. The love of husband for wife was measured, not by the physical delight or

spiritual fulfilment he might give her, but by security, material
sufficiency, social status. The love of wife for husband was measured, not by her power to lift him to heaven, but by her submission, her housewifely efficiency, her motherhood. The marriage
relationship was understood in social rather than in personal
terms, as a static rather than a dynamic conjunction, as objective
rather than subjective.

Romanticism blew this idea sky-high. Against the ready-made
institution of marriage, Romanticism set the subjective raptures,
the creative freedom, the heavenward aspiration of 'the grand
passion'. Against the permanence of the marriage-bond, Romanticism set the intensity of temporary liaisons, and claimed
the right to follow passion wherever it might lead. But the
understanding of marriage itself was also affected by this upsurge
of feeling, this demand for colour and emotional richness and
fulfilment. People began to look for more in marriage than the
social and legal definition had provided : they began to expect
a depth of personal feeling, a sense of rapture, an experience
of mutual sharing which went beyond the social and economic
relatedness of the married 'state'. Marriage, understood in this
Romantic sense, could no longer be a pre-existent paradigm.
It must be a relationship created by the lovers themselves
through their intersubjectivity, and no legal or ecclesiastical
formula could ensure its presence or guarantee its persistence.
Hence the rather startling conclusion of George Sand, 'The
increasing need for a divorce law arises from the higher order
of attraction between the sexes.'[19]

As H. G. Schenk remarks, many marriages have been enriched
by this Romantic intensification of love. But it is notoriously
difficult to maintain intensity of feeling, even intermittently,
throughout married life. This painful fact produces disappointment as deep as any that human beings can feel, and there is
much sadness in the decline of a relationship from passion and
devotion to conventionality and coldness. As we have seen, many
modern novelists view this decline as inevitable and present us
with heroes and heroines who claim the right to renew their
rapture with other, illegitimate, partners.

There is also the more extreme view that legitimatized sex is sex with most of the *frisson* taken out of it. Extra-marital sex becomes an important part of the individual protest against the pressures exerted by society. It may also be associated with political activity: in the modern novel it is almost axiomatic that men and women who are politically committed will sleep with each other. But when sex is made socially acceptable by marriage, it ceases to bear this quality of protest and becomes simply a piece of 'approved' conduct. It is therefore obvious that pronouncements by authorities about the wrongfulness of sex outside marriage merely increase its protest-value. And invocation of the highest Authority of all produces the additional excitement of turning a social or political protest into a metaphysical one.

6

The Romantic conviction that marriage is not a paradigm created by God but an inter-subjective relationship created by a man and a woman has modified but has not necessarily demolished traditional Christian teaching on this subject. The theological pillars of Christian marriage were understood to be the covenant-relationship between God and Israel in the Old Testament, and the love of Christ for the Church in the New Testament. Both of these implied total commitment and permanence. Moreover, by thus incorporating marriage into the scheme of divine redemption, Christianity firmly discouraged any hedonistic views about the married state and devalued the erotic element almost to vanishing point. The violent re-assertion of eroticism in this century by the successors of the Romantics has not left Christian views unaffected. There has been an admission of the hedonistic principle into the modern Christian estimate of marriage, as is indicated by the easing of the attitude of some Churches towards contraception, abortion, and divorce. It has become almost impossible to maintain the view that the married state is unaltered by failure of the personal relationship, and the Church recognizes that it has an important responsibility in helping couples to overcome such failure, though without so far feeling able to assert unreservedly that failure may sometimes be irremediable.

The danger is, of course, that any concession to the Romantic idea of love may lead inexorably to a total acceptance of its subjectivism. Already the view has been put forward by some Christian writers that love can legitimatize sexual relations without marriage if each partner earnestly desires the best for the other. Without wishing to deny that this may sometimes be true, I think that most social-workers and clergy would say that the view is naïve in that it credits people with greater emotional maturity and powers of self-understanding than they possess. More often than not, the 'love' in question turns out to be as deceptive as that depicted by Lynne Reid Banks in *The L-Shaped Room*.[20] The so-called 'new' morality is an attempt to understand relations between the sexes in terms of the fundamental Christian conviction that we are not under Law but under Grace, which is by no means the same thing as Romantic subjectivism. But it has failed to avoid giving the impression that an imprimatur has now been accorded to the kind of casual 'love' which is frequently presented in popular fiction.

What is, I think, certain is that the matrimonial chaos of our time, which fiction so clearly reflects, will not be ordered by attempts to re-establish the old paradigm. Modern man detests paradigms and strongly suspects that much of his malaise is due to their increasing domination of his life. What Christian teaching should assert is not that marriage is a way of regulating sexuality but rather that it is the means by which sexuality is liberated and sacramentalized. If any sense at all is to be made of the analogy between marriage and the relationship of Christ to the Church, it must surely be in terms of the *release* of love that we must understand it. What the New Testament is offering us here is not a paradigm but a *mystery* – a fully personal conjunction in which the depths of personhood are never exhausted but always disclose deeper mystery as its meaning unfolds. St Paul, who is not usually considered to be our best guide in matters matrimonial, rightly speaks of marriage as 'a great mystery', and it is in this 'mysteriousness' of the relationship that he sees the parallel with Christ and the Church. 'Mystery' does not stand for the unknowable: it stands for the inexhaustible. Marriage is able to admit us to the bottomless depths of personal being: knowledge of the other person does not dissipate the mystery, for the awareness of even greater mystery is always present as a quality of the known.[21] The *other* always transcends me: Sammy Mountjoy's mistake was to try to pluck out the heart of this mystery, to enter into immediate possession of that which may be had only by patient, humble exploration and even then is never wholly captured. The mystery of love lies in the fact that love is an unending process of discovery and has the power to create its object, to give reality to that which it desires to find. To attempt to possess the being of another immediately, without passing through the process of mutual creative discovery, is to grasp emptiness.

Within the human context we are poignantly aware of failure in love. The problem of *Under the Volcano* is that of the failure to be 'present' for the beloved, to have the heart and mind filled with memory and desire, yet to live in a solitary *now* which is both hated and cherished. T. S. Eliot expressed this poignancy in *The Waste Land*:

> April is the cruellest month, breeding
> Lilacs out of the dead land, mixing
> Memory and desire, stirring
> Dull roots with spring rain.[22]

Memory looks to the past and desire to the future: between them lies an empty present. Sometimes we can conceal from ourselves the emptiness or even come to resent intrusion, but the spring rain reminds us of our loss. How can the emptiness be filled? Eliot returns to this question in *The Dry Salvages* and points us to the Incarnation when he writes,

> Here the impossible union
> Of spheres of existence is actual,
> Here the past and the future
> Are conquered and reconciled . . .

Christ unites the 'spheres of existence': he correlates the outward reality with the inward dream, unites flesh with spirit and gives that continuity of presence by which the *now* of existence is made rich again. Human love belongs to the context of the creative Protest of Christ against all human alienation and the selfish concern by which it is promoted. Sexual pastimes do not overcome alienation: they merely confirm the sentence of solitary confinement, as anyone can see who observes the faces of the audience at a strip-tease show or a nudist film. The true protest is love, but it is the kind of love Eliot points to in the lines,

> No occupation either, but something given
> And taken, in a lifetime's death in love,
> Ardour and selflessness and self-surrender.[23]

We must think of marriage, not in terms of a received standard of social respectability, but in the context of this love. For marriage puts us in the way of the giving and receiving, the mutuality of aim and interest, the endless possibility of personal discovery, which are the main procedures by which human beings are able to protest against the solitude and triviality of their lives. As they make this protest, they are made aware of the presence of the Son of Man in whom the human context passes into the divine, and they find that the mystery of human relatedness is grounded in the mystery of God, who is 'the depth and ground of all our being' (Robinson). Moreover, the love created in marriage is not limited to the couple themselves – just as the love of Christ is not limited to the Church. It is creative of love beyond itself – in the children and friends and neighbours – following in this the pattern of the divine love which has no confines and stops at no terminus. The true freedom of love is found not in promiscuous intercourse but in the freedom to reach that depth of love in which humanity itself is grounded. The reality of love is known not only in the transfiguring experience of romantic passion but also in obligation, mutual caring and sacrifice – all those elements in marriage and in life which go against the grain of our selfish nature. For it is fundamentally against this nature that our protest must be made if we are to be released from our individual prisons into the freedom of love. The protest may well first express itself in a sense of rapture so intense as to make coldness unthinkable, but the fact is that the sustaining of it throughout life has more to do with the will than the emotions. No doubt the anti-romanticism of the

Duchess of Plaza-Toro went too far in the direction of cynicism, and her motive was certainly questionable, but she had something of the truth of the matter.

I said to myself, 'That man is a duke and I *will* love him.' Several of my relatives bet me I couldn't, but I did. Passionately.

Notes

1. George Orwell, *Nineteen Eighty-four*, Secker and Warburg, London 1949, Penguin Books and Harcourt, Brace & World, New York 1949.
2. Bizet's opera. The libretto is, of course, based on the story by Prosper Mérimée.
3. H. G. Schenk, *The Mind of the European Romantics*, Constable & Co., London 1966, p. 156.
4. There are useful accounts of Mozart's opera in A. Einstein, *Mozart*, Cassell & Co., London 1946, and E. Newman, *More Opera Nights*, Putnam & Co., London 1954.
5. E. Newman, *op. cit.*, p. 339.
6. *German Stories*, ed. Harry Steinhauer, Bantam Books 1961, p. 61.
7. E. Wilson, *Axel's Castle*, Scribners, New York 1942, pp. 262-4 and Collins Fontana Books, London 1961.
8. S. Kierkegaard, *Either/Or*, tr. Swenson, Princeton University Press 1944 and Anchor Books 1959, Vol. I, p. 88.
9. Ortega y Gasset, *The Modern Theme*, Harper Torch Books, New York 1961, p. 59.
10. T. Mann, *The Confessions of Felix Krull*, Secker and Warburg, London 1955, Penguin Books, 1958 and Alfred A. Knopf, New York 1955.
11. S. de Beauvoir, *Nature of the Second Sex*, tr. Parshley, Jonathan Cape, London 1953, Four-Square Books, 1963, pp. 190-1 and Alfred A. Knopf, New York 1953.
12. W. Golding, *Free Fall*, Faber & Faber, London 1959, Penguin Books, 1963 and Harcourt, Brace & World, New York 1960.
13. Goethe, *Faust Part II, Hymnus Mysticus*. These famous lines are given a choral setting by Liszt in 'A Faust Symphony' and by Mahler in his Symphony No. 8.
14. M. Lowry, *Under the Volcano*, Jonathan Cape, London 1947, Penguin Books, 1962 and Reynal & Hitchcock, New York 1947.
15. J. P. Donleavy, *The Ginger Man*, Corgi Books, London 1963 and Random House, New York 1961.
16. S. de Beauvoir, *op. cit.*
17. B. Brophy, *The Snow Ball*, Corgi Books, London 1966.
18. I. Murdoch, *A Severed Head*, Chatto and Windus, London 1961, Penguin Books, 1963 and Viking Press, New York 1961.
19. Quoted by H. G. Schenk, *op. cit.*, p. 158.

20. Lynne Reid Banks, *The L-Shaped Room*, Chatto and Windus, London 1960, Penguin Books, 1962 and Simon & Schuster, New York 1961.

21. J. Pelikan, *The Christian Intellectual*, Collins, London 1966, p. 76 and Harper & Row, New York 1966.

22. T. S. Eliot, *The Waste Land*, in *Collected Poems, 1909-62*, Faber & Faber, London 1963 and Harcourt, Brace & World, New York 1963.

23. T. S. Eliot, *The Dry Salvages*, in *Collected Poems, 1909-62*.

8

Nostalgia for the Primates

It is a serious question today whether Don Juanism is possible. This is not merely a question about our social arrangements: it is a question about man. To those who find credible the vulgar Juanistic fantasies of fictional life, the answer may seem obvious. L'homme moyen sensuel, it is supposed, would readily close with the Juanistic deal and would count himself on Fortune's cap the very button. But the question is not so easily disposed of. What we are asking is whether it is possible for man to live altogether outside the range of personal and ethical categories. Can he recover an 'innocence' which will enable him to live a life of unreflecting enjoyment in the kingdom of the sensuous, or must he find that such a life is, in the end, denied by his own nature?

Kierkegaard thought that the unconquerable enemy of Don Juanism was reflection. When reflection enters the kingdom of the sensuous, he said, it appears as the kingdom of sin, and by that time Don Juan is slain. Thus Don Juanism is not a possible attitude for a being who cannot help asking questions about his life and who knows that his innocence is irretrievably lost. 'To exist as a human being,' says Kierkegaard, 'is to exist ethically,' and Don Juanism must itself be brought under ethical categories if it is to play its part as one of 'the three great ideas' in the formation of man.*

An 'ethical' Don Juan – as an actual human being, that is, as distinct from the *idea* of Don Juanism – is impossible, but it

* 'The three great ideas (Don Juan, Faust and the Wandering Jew) represent, as it were, life outside religion in its three-fold direction, and only when those ideas are merged in the individual and become mediate, only then do morals and religion appear; that is my view of those three ideas in relation to my dogmatic standpoint.' *Journal* 1836.

may be that a reflective Don Juan is not. His way of life may be based on a specific philosophy. He may have reflected upon ethical values and decided that they are illusory and inimical to happiness. He may have come to the conclusion that there is no mysterious infinitude in personal life, no rich manifold, no transcendence in which the individual finds himself surpassed. And in the light of this conclusion he may have chosen his vocation as the only reasonable option in a meaningless world. He knows what the limits are and does not go beyond them. In an absurd world there is no question of personal guilt since there are no criteria by which human actions can be judged. In such a world it is necessary to seize the immediate joy of the moment and to live in terms neither of regret nor of hope. Life is without a yesterday and without a tomorrow, and to ponder its 'meaning' is to lose the opportunities of today.

Such is the understanding of Don Juan presented by Albert Camus. Juan is a type of the absurd man whose special characteristic is his inability to believe in 'the deep meaning of things'. The point about Juan is not that he is an unreflecting womanizer but that he has a lucid consciousness of the limits within which happiness lies. He finds sufficiency in what is and refuses to hope for what might be. Hope, says Camus, is relevant only for 'the men of eternity', and men who live in hope 'accommodate themselves badly to this world'. But the life of Don Juan is perfectly accommodated to this world because, like the world itself, it is sterile.[1]

Camus's Don Juan is not 'innocent'. He has decided to live as if he were innocent, which is a very different thing. Such a choice is already reflective, already rational, and the life thus chosen must at least sometimes be beset by the alternatives which the choice has excluded. No doubt it is true that man is 'penetrated by the absurd', as Camus says, but it is no less true that he is penetrated by a sense of moral realities – which may, indeed, be ignored, but which cannot simply be excluded from consciousness by an initial choice. The philosophy of the absurd makes all purposive action – including the choice of absurdity itself – impossible. If, as Camus suggests, consciousness of the absurd makes all actions equal, then there can be no basis for choosing anything at all and life becomes a mere succession of random impulses. 'In spite of its defence of the value of consciousness,' says Philip Thody, '*Le Mythe de Sisyphe* is, like *L'Etranger*, a nihilistic book: there is no suggestion that any action can be either praised or blamed on moral grounds, that man can be held responsible for the consequences of his acts, no possibility that words like duty, self-sacrifice, charity or generosity can have any meaning.'[2]

As we saw in chapter five, Camus moved away from this position in *The Plague* and *The Rebel*. He did so by trying to fit a philosophy of revolt into his philosophy of the absurd. I have suggested that the two philosophies are inconsistent with each other: there is no reason for being a healer in an absurd world, and Camus was right when he said in *Le Mythe de Sisyphe* that in such a world we can be virtuous only by accident. But *The Plague* shows that there *are* moral values: the whole novel can be read as a passionate protest against totalitarian political systems which are founded on murder and outrage. The philosophy of the absurd cannot account for the existence of the categorical imperative which summons men to revolt against human suffering; on the contrary, the fact that the world contains this imperative must be counted as evidence against absurdity. It must also make untenable the view that man can choose 'innocence'.

2

'Anyone who has meditated a good deal on man, by profession or vocation, is led to feel nostalgia for the primates. They at least don't have any ulterior motives.' Camus puts those words into the mouth of Jean-Baptiste Clamence, the hero of his later novel *The Fall*, but it is hard to resist the conviction that the opinion thus humorously expressed is Camus's own. There is in his writings a persisting recurrence of the theme of human innocence, of nostalgia for the joys of immediacy, undistracted by hope or regret. This nostalgia is closely related to the happiness of Camus's youth in Algeria, which he recreated in his story *Noces* where he describes the delight of simply being alive to lie in the sun and swim in the sea of a Mediterranean summer. Nature is indifferent to the strife of men – an idea which comes out again in Meursault's desire to surrender himself to 'the benign indifference of the universe' – and a sense of nature as a source of spiritual cleansing occurs in *The Plague* when Rieux and Tarrou go for a swim in the sea and rid themselves for a short time of the pestilence. Clamence in *The Fall* longs for 'the sun, beaches and islands in the path of the trade winds, youth whose memory drives me to despair', while Janine, in *La Femme Adultère*, is able to forget the alienation of age in a sense of harmony with the sky and stars which is almost sexual in its intensity.[3]

This feeling of a secret innocence which, for Camus, humanity has never quite lost, goes far to explain the most striking characteristic of his thought – his demand for 'limits', for moderation, his refusal of fanaticism and the dogmatic certainties by which men are able to justify torture and murder. It may be argued that his philosophy of man sometimes seems to be over-simplified and idealistic, that it fails to take into full account the self-centred evil of the human heart. But the opposite error can also be made, and it is hard to disagree with Camus in his belief that 'no attitude can be so absolutely true as to deserve our complete allegiance' (Thody). Camus would not deny – indeed he asserts – the 'pestiferousness' of man: he knows very well that man repudiates his innocence and turns to power, to the desire to dominate, to justify his existence; if man would only realize that he has 'nothing to justify', he could be happy again.

It must be admitted, however, that there is a certain ambiguity in Camus's treatment of man as a moral agent. This is noticeable in *The Plague*. In the early chapters, Camus spends some time in describing the day-by-day lives of the citizens of Oran and shows them to be as senseless as the plague itself. The people are 'sunk in stupid human confidence', and the onset of the plague has the salutary effect of compelling them to question their own unthinking complacency. This didactic effect of the plague is never quite lost sight of in the novel: there may even be said to be a sense in which the priest is right when he claims that the epidemic is a judgment on human sin, and at the very end of the story Rieux reminds himself that the plague will come again 'for the bane and enlightening of men'. But against this there is also the idea – and perhaps it is the dominating one – that man is the innocent victim of an evil which is wholly external to him. The most important incident here is the death of the little boy: he at least, says Rieux, was innocent, and Rieux is surely speaking for Camus himself when he says that he will for ever refuse to accept a universe in which the innocent are tortured. Throughout the novel one feels the intensity of Camus's sympathy for ordinary people, who may indeed have lost the innocence of childhood but whose guilt can never merit the monstrous tyranny of a hideous death. It is hard to disagree with this verdict, and the fact that the problem is a very old one which has called forth many attempts to justify God is hardly a sufficient answer to Camus's agonized question. One cannot help feeling that Camus has shown that all theodicies are in the end nothing but callous sophistry.

If *The Plague* were merely about external evil for which man is not responsible, we should have to concede that Camus had made his point. But we have noticed that this is not so. The disease is also meant to be a symbol of the evil in man, and it is a weakness of the novel that microbes are very inadequate symbols of human motives. The plague bacillus creates no moral conflict: it must simply be opposed and eliminated. The matter is clear-cut and the appropriate human action is obvious to any reasonable man. But if the plague represents the evil element *in* man – the desire to dominate, for example – then moral conflict must arise and the problem of appropriate action will become incomparably more complex. The weakness of *The Plague* is that it tries to treat the latter kind of case as though it were the former kind, with the result that the moral ambiguity of human motives is hard to fit into the framework of the parable. The difference may be illustrated from a recent article in which a B.B.C. correspondent, René Cutforth, described his experience in Algeria during the fight for independence. As is well known, atrocities were committed on both sides, and Cutforth mentions scenes of horror 'inconceivable except by the insane or the patriotic' – as, for example, women tied up in chairs and their

children left on their laps to die slowly of knife wounds. But in
the same period occurred the earthquake at Agadir on the coast
of Morocco, and Cutforth was sent there from Algeria to get
the story. He describes how an international team of three
thousand worked for days amid the stench of rotting corpses to
free the victims still trapped under tons of rubble.[4] The plague
in Camus's novel is like the earthquake at Agadir, and Rieux
would have been happy there 'doing his job'. But while men
were rescuing the victims in Agadir, other men were doing those
other things in Algeria. Rieux would not have found his job
quite as straightforward there. The 'patriots' would have wanted
to know whose side he was on.

It is impossible to achieve personal sanctity, with or without
God, in a world which does not offer unambiguous moral choices.
Our very existence is a kind of 'fall' into unfulfilled potential
in which there are no hard outlines and no escape from the
anxiety which conditions all our becoming. Christ himself was
not exempt from the tragic destiny which marks all genuinely
human existence. To seek to abstract oneself from a sinful world
in order to cultivate a detached rectitude is to be guilty of what
Berdyaev called a transcendent egoism. It turns out that the
pursuit of individual moral integrity is itself morally blame-
worthy, and may even be a subtle way of achieving that very
sense of domination which, in its overt political forms for example, we righteously condemn. It is to this problem that Camus
turns his attention in *The Fall*.

3

Jean-Baptiste Clamence is a Paris lawyer whose delight is to
plead for the orphan, the widow, and other drop-outs from
society. He is a kind of legal equivalent of Dr Rieux. He domin-
ates by his virtue. He takes special pleasure in helping the blind
to cross the road, giving up his seat on the train, bestowing
generous alms upon beggars, and so on. He even attends the
funeral of his concierge, a man of malice and rancour 'who would
have discouraged a Franciscan'. All in all, Clamence lives a life
of splendid impregnability: his moral superiority enables him,

in the guise of helping the weak, to live 'surtout', to place himself at a summit of rectitude from which he can look down with
irony and contempt upon the human race. He confesses to a
liking for living high up, especially on an island where it is
possible to dominate the whole scene from a suitably chosen
vantage point. His perfection and his contentment are complete.

Three events occur which bring down Clamence from his
moral height. As he is crossing a bridge he hears laughter
behind him, but no one is there. He is humiliated by an incident
at traffic-lights. And he merely walks on when a girl throws herself into the Seine. The collapse of his self-esteem leads him to
abandon his legal practice in Paris and to take up residence in
Amsterdam where he installs himself in a new profession – that
of 'judge-penitent'.

The question for Clamence is how to rise again after his fall.
How can he regain his position of domination? His new profession is the answer. By confessing his own sins he is able to
induce in his listener a sense of guilt. Every judge, he points
out, eventually ends up as a penitent, so the best procedure is
to reverse this order 'and practise the profession of penitent to
be able to end up as a judge'. Clamence's guilty portrait of
himself thus becomes a mirror in which his contemporaries see
their own reflections. His confession passes imperceptibly from
'I' to 'we', and before they realize it his audience are condemn-
ing, not Clamence, but themselves. At this point Clamence can
move from the role of penitent to that of judge. All are in the
soup together, but Clamence has the superiority of knowing it
and this gives him the right to speak. 'You see the advantage, I
am sure.'

The Fall is a witty, urbane, ironical book. It is also very
funny. There are many exposures of attitudes which such public
guardians as politicians, judges and clergymen would do well
to ponder. The difficulty, however, is to know where irony ends
and seriousness begins. What attitude, if any, is Camus com-
mending?

I think we are meant to take seriously Clamence's discovery
that his life of virtue is fraudulent. His 'fall' is not a decline
from moral eminence : it is a painful recognition of the fact that

he has been living in a fool's paradise, unaware that in reality he cares nothing for the poor but is simply using them as a device for self-adulation. When the real test comes he is found wanting, and nothing can ever be the same again. Clamence cannot ignore 'the dissonances and disorder' that now fill him. He cannot forget that he failed to help the girl who drowned herself. His first reaction is to play the Don Juan, to try to throw off his guilt in enjoyment of a succession of incurious ladies. But Camus makes it clear that he no longer regards Juanistic 'innocence' as a possible option for an ethical human being. Clamence's memory of guilt remains, ready to spring back into consciousness when he least expects it – just as, we remember, the plague bacillus will lie hidden for years and then suddenly 'rouse up its rats again'. The 'judge-penitent' describes how, long after the Seine incident, he had been on an ocean liner – 'on the upper deck of course' – looking out over the sea. Suddenly he had caught sight of a black speck on the water: it had only been a piece of debris, but for a moment it had seemed like a drowning man. And Clamence had realized then that the cry which had sounded over the Seine had travelled with him wherever he had gone and would continue to wait for him 'on seas and rivers, everywhere, in short, where lies the bitter water of my baptism'.

There is no irony here: it is fully meant, and is indeed a poignant reminder of the human condition, of the irrecoverable loss of innocence, the memory of the evil deed which each of us carries in his heart and which no choice can ever eliminate from our deepest awareness. The absurd man for whom all actions are equal is not a credible human being. We cannot forget the past, and there is no second chance – 'fortunately', says Clamence, because of course we would fail again – to retrieve our lost integrity. We have become 'pestiferous': we have learnt that even our best actions carry infection. Each of us has to 'submit and confess his guilt'; each of us has to live in the 'little-ease' where we can neither stand up nor lie down.

Clamence's way of living with his guilt is to confess it in such a fashion as to make his confession an accusation of others. Thus he recovers his superiority. But here Camus' intention is clearly ironical. No doubt it is better to be a judge-penitent than to lay claim to a bogus virtue, but even Clamence seems to view his new profession with a sardonic eye and admits that he is a 'false prophet'. As an exposure of the kind of evangelism which purveys its gospel, political or religious, by trading on feelings of guilt, Camus's judge-penitent performs a useful service: he shows that confessions and elicitations of guilt can be devices by means of which the evangelist gratifies his urge to dominate. But as a serious answer to Clamence's genuine agony, his new profession is a non-starter. Clamence has merely exchanged one self-deception for another. His real problem remains unsolved.

As Philip Thody points out, *The Fall* to some extent corrects or at least modifies the views expressed in *The Plague* and *The Rebel*: in the person of Clamence, Camus recognizes and grapples with the impurity of human motives. Man is no longer, it would seem, the innocent victim of circumstance or the innocent dupe of tyrants. Even his most 'disinterested' actions are prompted by self-regarding aims; the desire to dominate is never absent, perhaps least of all from the man who lays claim to virtue, and our readiness to accuse others reveals our own bad consciences. It looks as if Camus has given up his belief in man's essential innocence.

I would suggest, however, that this is not altogether the case. It is certainly a mistake to suppose, as some have been all too ready to do, that in *The Fall* Camus shows himself to be a convert to the orthodox Christian doctrine of original sin. Camus has not abandoned his theory of limits: excessive claims to virtue and excessive accusations of guilt are both disastrous, leading inevitably to tyranny and servitude. Man is not wholly innocent, and Clamence's recognition of the presence of self-regarding motives in his life of virtue is an advance on Rieux's simplistic morality of 'doing his job'. But to swing as Clamence does to the opposite extreme of unremitting self-denunciation is to forget that there are also limits to guilt. Camus is suggesting that denial of man's *relative* innocence is as catastrophic as denial of his relative wickedness. The guilty man comforts himself by involving others in his guilt: 'we are all in the soup together', he says. But there is no deliverance in this mutual accusation: no problems are solved when we merely spit in each other's faces. Neither in personal life nor in international diplomacy does cold war create peace. All men are guilty – or 'pestiferous', to use Tarrou's word – but we do not overcome the disabling effect of guilt by denouncing ourselves or accusing others. What, then, is the alternative?

I think Camus is implying that, although we are guilty, our only hope lies in our being treated *as if we were innocent*. He is hinting at something that is surprisingly like the doctrine of grace. 'God's sole usefulness,' says Clamence, 'would be to guarantee innocence, and I am inclined to see religion as a huge laundering venture – as it was once, but briefly, for exactly three years, and it wasn't called religion.' The trouble is that 'religion' has forgotten its origins and has become guilt-ridden and unforgiving. The Lord has been hoisted on to the judge's bench – we judge others 'in his name'.

> He spoke softly to the adulteress: 'Neither do I condemn thee.' But that doesn't matter; they condemn without absolving anyone. In the name of the Lord, here is what you deserve. Lord? He, my friend, didn't expect so much. He simply wanted to be loved, nothing more. Of course, there are those who love him, even among Christians. But they are not numerous (p. 85).

Against the judgmental attitude which the Church has so often deployed against the world, Camus rightly sets the forgiving love of 'the first Christian'.* It is the heart of the Gospel that God in Christ treats us as if we were innocent, that he accepts us as we are, with our guilt, because only so can the entail of the past be broken. Camus sees that this is the only exit from the crushing morality of merit and desert, but he has failed to notice the emphasis of the New Testament on the cost and sacrifice which made it possible. The conclusion which Clamence seems to draw from the Gospel is the optimistic one that human guilt is not, after all, a very serious matter – a view which is very much in line with Camus's idea of the secret 'innocence' of man which we have noticed in his earlier books. Jesus forgave – 'he simply wanted to be loved', says Clamence. But this is to offer

---

*This is Clamence's rather revealing way of referring to Christ.

us the Gospel without its moral astringency and to reduce Jesus
to an impotent sentimentalist. Jesus was not merely an ill-used
lover of men who could not bear to live with the human guilt
in which he shared : he died *for* our sin – not, as Camus says, in
order to escape from it. We are accepted not because we *are*
innocent but in spite of the fact that we are not, and in this
difference lies the whole deadly serious moral necessity which
required that Jesus should suffer and die. It is not true that for
man 'there is nothing to justify'. What *is* true, as Camus, almost
in spite of himself, has shown, is that man cannot justify himself. God therefore treats him as innocent; but he does so, not by
ignoring sin and thereby reducing moral values to meaninglessness and making forgiveness superfluous, but by absorbing our
evil deeds into himself on Calvary. This is the truth behind the
sometimes crudely expressed doctrine of 'penal substitution'. It is
not that God punishes the innocent Jesus in order to satisfy some
non-personal necessity of his moral nature, but rather that in
Christ he accepts for himself the dislocation of personal life,
the self-accusing alienation, which is what moral failure is
about. No one who has glimpsed the meaning of the cry of
dereliction can assent to Camus's optimism. The measure of
human sin is there shown to be no less than its power to separate
the Son of God from his Heavenly Father, to cause a kind of
fracture in the divine life. Calvary is the terrible place where
guilt is stripped of all its sophistries. But it is also the place where
love accepts guilt in order that the saving passion may be
released.

Writing of *The Fall*, Philip Thody remarks that 'the hardest
trial for any humanist is to admit that man is cruel, hypocritical
and self-centred and yet not despair in him'. He thinks that
Camus faces up to this trial. But for all the shrewdness of its
insights and the clarity of its language, *The Fall* is finally a
disappointing book : it offers only an ironical commentary on
a serious human question. We are left with a false prophet, and
the solution to the problem of human guilt seems to vanish into
the rain and fog of Amsterdam where the judge-penitent carries
on his profession. Perhaps Camus is simply saying that there *is*
no solution and that we must be content to live ambiguously in

the strange half-light between guilt and innocence without claiming virtue and without losing heart. This is an attractive, almost
Epicurean view, and probably most of us are able to live by it
for most of the time. But it does not help us 'in the sombre
season or the sudden fury', and it is hard to see how it can
include the kind of challenge and sacrifice which made Camus's
earlier imperative of revolt so exhilarating. There are limits to
the living of life within limits. For a study of life at extremes,
beyond the Camusian limits, we return to the work of another
writer – William Golding.

4

Golding is primarily concerned to trace back the travails of
human existence to their source in human nature and to repudiate the idea that something other than man himself is
responsible for failure. In thus fastening responsibility on man
Golding shares a view which we have noticed in the writings
of Kafka and Sartre, though his findings are more pessimistic
than theirs. It is not 'nothingness' that lies at the centre of man's
being but an actively evil principle. No man ever achieves an
integrated moral consciousness and no human enterprise is
free from distortion. The lesson of *The Spire* is that man is
most pathetic when he fails to recognize this and claims for
himself a moral purity which belongs only to God. To this
danger 'religious' man is especially exposed because he all too
easily begins to think that his schemes and judgments are
divinely originated and are therefore above criticism. We may
recall here that not even St Paul was free from this error, to
say nothing of many lesser men in the course of church history.
There are also parallels in the claims of political messianism,
and we have noticed in this connection the warning of Camus
that absolutist pretensions are deathly, however worthy their
theoretical aims may be. We may also recollect Kafka's liken-
ing of those who try to attain exhaustive knowledge of the
decrees of the High Command to a river which forgets its proper
limits and overflows its banks. These warnings and parables may
be said to be indications of areas in the modern estimate of man

where there is an overlap with the estimate presented in the myths of the Book of Genesis. But it is, I think, in the work of Golding that the overlap is explicit.

Golding once described the true business of the novelist as 'an Aeschylean preoccupation with the human tragedy', defined as a commitment to 'looking for the root of the disease instead of describing the symptoms'.[5] It has long been recognized that this was also the purpose of those who fashioned the stories of Adam and Eve, Cain and Abel, and the Tower of Babel, and there is little doubt that Golding had these stories in mind when writing his novels. We may notice, first, that Golding reproduces the technique of the Genesis myths in his usual practice of isolating his characters from contemporary social and cultural structures. The protective wrapping must be torn off before the inner reality of man can be exposed. Like the Genesis myths Golding points to the tragic element in human life and attempts to probe down to its causes. He thinks that the only hope of overcoming the evil in our nature is by clarity in recognizing and stating its presence, and by vigilance in keeping watch on our actions and the motives by which they are prompted.

Golding's novels are also comparable to the Genesis myths in the sense they give of man's *helplessness* as he recognizes the presence of a destructive element in himself. Here there is a marked contrast with those optimistic diagnoses of the human condition and the correspondingly optimistic assessment of human ability to deal with it which characterized much theological thinking before 1914 and is also typical of humanist thinking today. As an example of the latter, we may instance Dennis Gabor's *Inventing the Future*. He makes the point – and one cannot help sympathizing with it – that it is easy to be a prophet of doom and to spread alarm and despondency about the future of the human race. What man now requires is a new confidence in himself, a realization that he possesses the knowledge and the skill to 'invent' his own destiny.

Man will become the object of science not just for providing him with comforts, not just for curing him of ailments, but for reshaping his heredity at a pace incomparably faster than sluggish natural evolution.[6]

For the first time on this planet, a being has appeared which can determine its own biological advance. Soon men will no longer be the passive objects of natural processes, but will have learnt how to harness and control those processes and to breed the kind of humanity they want. At the limit of speculation along this line of thought, Gabor pictures the English being able to 'breed back' to Shakespeare and Newton, the Italians to Leonardo and Michelangelo. At a less extreme limit, Gabor sees a natural emergence of happy and healthy beings when science has at last succeeded in making the struggle for survival 'less murderous'. In the eudaemonistic paradise, there will no longer be a place or an occupation for the great tortured artists of the past – the Beethovens, the Dostoevskys, the Flauberts – whose creative genius thrived on the tragic conflicts of human life. Tragic conflicts will no longer exist, and the pessimistic estimate of man, which has to be maintained in order that tragic art may be created, will be abandoned.

Does this mean that there will be no great creators in the happy humanity of the future? Gabor points us to Mozart as 'a creator fit to live in Arcady'. Mozart's life was short, hard and tragic, but 'his work owes nothing to his sufferings, everything to his innate rich and happy nature'. He was 'a forerunner of Mozartian Man, of the creator whose art does not live on conflict, who creates for joy, out of joy'. Gabor says that 'he prefers to disbelieve those who want to make a neurotic of Mozart', and it may even be that in the joyful future of the simple man and woman, Mozarts may be born again.[7]

In thinking that the creators of tragic art have a kind of vested interest in maintaining a pessimistic estimate of man, Gabor may be right. We have already noticed the tendency of existentialist writers to absolutize the Absurd, and we ought to be on our guard against confusing the kind of thing a particular writer happens to do well, because of his private neurosis, with what is 'genuinely human'. But one cannot help feeling that Gabor's citation of Mozart works against his hypothesis rather than in favour of it. If Mozart was not neurotic – and Gabor is surely right when he says that no one has ever reacted less neurotically to an archiepiscopal kick in the pants –

how are we to explain the fact that so many people have detected tragic depths in his music? The G minor symphony, songs in the operas like *Dove sono* and *Ach, ich fühl's* which seem to speak of a sadness more permanent than the circumstances suggest, cannot be said to have been created 'out of joy'. Even when the words are happy, as in *Bei Männern*, Mozart's music seems to feel them in a way which reminds us of the sadness which always underlies our contentment.* May it not be that this 'tragic sense of life' is after all deeper than neurosis and more constant than a passing stage of evolution?

5

In contrast with doctrines such as that of Gabor which would make man's moral ease wholly dependent upon his psychological balance and his freedom from irksome toil, both of which are theoretically attainable, Golding posits a mystifying and inescapable irrationality in the human heart which erupts into violence, fear and selfish pride. The 'Lord of the Flies' is not Beelzebub, the prince of devils: he is part of the human race and cannot be cast out.

> 'There isn't anyone to help you. Only me. And I'm the Beast.'
> Simon's mouth laboured, brought forth audible words. 'Pig's head on a stick.'
> 'Fancy thinking the Beast was something you could hunt and kill!' said the head.
> For a moment or two the forest and all the other dimly appreciated places echoed with the parody of laughter.
> 'You knew, didn't you? I'm part of you. Close, close, close! I'm the reason why it's no go? Why things are what they are?'[8]

What is it that is 'no go'? It is the attempt to live under a rule of law and reason, to maintain civilized standards, to send out signals to another world in the hope of being 'saved'. All these efforts are nullified by a reversion to violence and barbarism. At the end of the novel, Ralph weeps for 'the end of innocence, the darkness of man's heart'.

* Cf. Barth's comments on Mozart's 'pessimism' in his essay *Wolfgang Amadeus Mozart* in *Religion and Culture*, ed. Walter Leibrecht, SCM Press, 1959.

Lord of the Flies is a complex version of the story of Cain – the man whose smoke-signal failed and who murdered his brother. Above all, it is a refutation of optimistic theologies which believed that God had created a world in which man's moral development had advanced *pari passu* with his biological evolution and would continue so to advance until an all-justifying End was reached.[9] What we have in *Lord of the Flies* is not moral achievement but moral regression. And there is no all-justifying End: the rescue-party which takes the boys off their island comes from a world in which regression has occurred on a gigantic scale – the scale of atomic war. The human plight is presented in terms which are unqualified and unrelieved. Cain is not merely our remote ancestor: he is contemporary man, and his murderous impulses are equipped with unlimited destructive power.

We may want to argue that no *general* conclusions about the human condition can properly be drawn from *Lord of the Flies*. Golding has started with a private theory about Man and has then provided some imaginary and highly selective evidence to support it. The novel has been called a 'fable' – a story told to enforce a moral lesson rather than to portray the rough, ambiguous actualities of human life. Sometimes we are rather too conscious that the author is nudging us as we read lest we fail to notice his doctrine of Man. The question that occurs to us is how imaginary events can be evidence for anything except the author's personal views.

I think the answer to this is that Golding succeeds in giving convincing form to that which exists deep in our self-awareness. By the skill of his writing he takes us step by step along the same regressive route as that traversed by the boys on the island. At first, we share Ralph's conviction that reason and order must be maintained; we also share Jack's initial feeling of repugnance at the thought of killing a pig – the knife 'descending and cutting into living flesh'. Our first reactions are those of 'civilized' people. But as the story continues, we find ourselves being caught up in the thrill of the hunt and the exhilaration of slaughter and blood and the whole elemental feeling of the island and the sea. As the boys decline from civilization into savagery, we decline with them and feel bored with Ralph's priggish worries about the smoke-signal. The depth of our identification may be assessed by the feeling of surprise we have when, at the end of the book, Golding makes us see the boys from the point of view of an uninvolved adult. To the naval officer, Ralph is 'a kid who needs a bath, a hair-cut, a nose-wipe, and a good deal of ointment', while Jack, the horrifying hunter, is 'a little boy who wore the remains of an extraordinary black cap'. We had thought of the boys as adults because we had seen ourselves in them. The backing of Golding's thesis comes not from the imaginary events on the island but from the reality of our response to them. Our minds turn to the outrages of our century – the slaughter of the first war, the concentration camps and atom-bombs of the second – and we realize that Golding has compelled us to acknowledge that there is in each of us a hidden recess which horrifyingly declares our complicity in torture and murder.

The most appalling event in *Lord of the Flies* is the murder of Simon. It is Simon who attains the true *gnosis*, who discovers the truth about the Beast – which is that there is no Beast other than the evil in the human mind. Simon is brave enough to go close to the supposed Beast and he then finds out what it really is – a dead airman whose body is raised into a sitting position and then lowered again by the wind playing in his parachute. Simon releases the trapped harness and a powerful gust of wind carries the corpse out to sea. Armed now with saving knowledge, Simon hastens back to tell the others – only to be set upon by the hunters and torn to pieces as he is attempting to deliver his message. We are reminded of a Redeemer who conquered demons and offered men knowledge of salvation, only to be scourged and nailed to a cross by the people he had come to save. The truth about Man is not merely that he is savage and afraid, but that he refuses deliverance and murders the messengers of light.

6

It might be thought that Golding's theory concerning the origin of moral evil is, after all, an evolutionary theory – in the sense that evil is thought to be the persistence in man of pre-rational drives belonging to his animal ancestry which further development will eliminate. Perhaps Golding was deliberately setting out to repudiate this view in the novel which followed *Lord of the Flies* entitled *The Inheritors*. This may be read as Golding's version of the Fall, with Neanderthal Man playing the part of prelapsarian Adam and Eve.[10]

Neanderthal Man was possibly the immediate predecessor of *homo sapiens*, and in the epigraph of his novel Golding quotes the description of him by H. G. Wells, in which he is said to have been hairy, ugly, repulsive, and possibly cannibalistic. As we read the novel we soon discover that Golding intends this epigraph in an ironical sense, for he presents Neanderthal Man as childlike and innocent, entirely free from the ferocious characteristics of Wells's description. The assumption of the Wellsian theory is that behind *homo sapiens* there was a primitive monster lacking all qualities of self-control, civilization and moral goodness. Golding attempts to show that the predecessor of *homo sapiens* was on the contrary a lover of Nature, of children, of animals, that he cared for the old and self-sacrificingly nurtured the young, that he would not take life and ate flesh only when an animal died from natural causes. Golding's imaginative power and literary skill persuade us as we read that his version of Neanderthal Man could be true, and our minds fill with echoes of our primal innocence and our lost Edens.

The evil influence in Golding's Eden is not a serpent but *homo sapiens* himself. The 'new people', as the Neanderthalers call him, are capable of rational speech and action: they have developed rudimentary techniques and mastered the skill of co-ordination of effort. But along with this has come cruelty, the urge to kill, and a sense of guilt which requires propitiatory offerings. In short, Golding is telling us that the Fall is to be understood, not in terms of primitive animalism, but as a concomitant of the rational consciousness itself. *Homo sapiens* is fallen from birth because moral evil is the other aspect of intellectual power. There is no need to posit some special act in order to account for the fall of man: moral evil is the price man must pay for his rationality and his creative imagination. It follows that there is no ground in man himself for hope of goodness; evolutionary progressivism is a delusion. At the very end of the novel, Golding shows us Tuami, a human being, peering across the water into the darkness beyond. But 'he could not see if the line of darkness had an ending'.

In *The Inheritors* we are even more conscious of the fabulous nature of Golding's creation than in *Lord of the Flies*. It is doubtful whether Neanderthal Man in fact exhibited the primal innocence Golding ascribes to him, and there is, it would seem, a distinct possibility that the Neanderthalers were not the predecessors of *homo sapiens*, but his contemporaries over a long period. However, as Clifford Geertz has remarked in an essay on Lévi-Strauss, perhaps 'every man has a right to create his own savage for his own purposes'.[11] Just as the biblical story of Adam and Eve does not stand or fall by its historical validity, so Golding's novel does not stand or fall by its anthropological exactness. With considerable skill, Golding has recreated a precognitive innocence, not in our remote ancestors, but in ourselves. He has shown us what it feels like to be unaware of moral evil, what it is like to have as the content of the mind a succession of unrelated pictures instead of a connected sequence of words, what it is like to have little or no skill in mastering environment. It is not really Neanderthal Man that Golding describes, but *homo sapiens* himself in that recess of his being where he remembers the innocence which he knows he has lost. The point is made clearer in the later novel, *Free Fall*, where the whole problem of guilt and servitude is made contemporary by being concentrated in one twentieth-century individual, who searches his life to find the place where he fell from innocence and lost his freedom.

One commentator on *The Inheritors* remarks that the novel is 'a blazingly heretical version of the Paradisal legend' because it presents man himself, not the serpent, as the tempter. But Golding's version is heretical only in terms of later interpretations of the Fall narrative in which the serpent was identified with the devil. The story itself has no such identification, and modern biblical scholars have rejected it. The serpent may be better understood, not as an external source of evil, but as a projection of the human mind. It represents man's questioning, experimental intelligence. A recent writer who takes this line is John Hick in his book *Evil and the God of Love*, where he says that 'the serpent is the first scientist; and the Fall is the first and most daring experiment'.[12] Perhaps we feel like remarking that the scientist has been blamed for a good many of the troubles of our time and that it seems a little hard to blame him even for the Fall. But Hick's point is, of course, that in a sense *all* men are 'scientists' because all must to some extent apply rational intelligence to Nature in order that environment may be mastered. In itself, says Hick, this urge is morally neutral, but it has evil consequences because 'in thus turning his primary attention upon the world as an environing order (man) forfeits the vision of God' and directs himself exclusively 'towards the absorbing task of mastering a largely hostile environment'. This task inevitably produces competitiveness and the lust of power which are the beginnings of moral evil. From seeking mastery over Nature, man turns to mastery over his fellows and sooner or later murders his own brother.

In *The Inheritors* Golding is thus in accord with at least some modern interpretations of the Fall when he implies that moral evil springs from the power of rational consciousness. The glory of man and the degradation of man are combined in paradox, and there is no means of knowing in advance which side of the paradox will dominate. Even at the highest level of his spiritual aspiration, man remains within the paradox. It is to this level that Golding turns his attention in *The Spire*.

Notes

1. *Le Mythe de Sisyphe*, p. 96.
2. P. Thody, *Albert Camus 1913-1960*, Hamish Hamilton, London 1961 and The Macmillan Co., New York 1962, p. 61.

3. Albert Camus, *Exile and the Kingdom*, Hamish Hamilton, London 1958, Penguin Books 1962 and Alfred A. Knopf, New York 1958.

4. René Cutforth, 'Agadir' in *The Listener*, 22 August 1968.

5. Quoted in *William Golding's Lord of the Flies. a Source Book*, ed. W. Nelson, Odyssey Press, New York 1963.

6. D. Gabor, *Inventing the Future*, Secker and Warburg, London 1963, p. 176 and Alfred A. Knopf, New York 1964.

7. Gabor, *op. cit.*, p. 180.

8. W. Golding, *Lord of the Flies*, Faber & Faber, London 1954, Penguin Books, 1960, p. 137 and Coward-McCann, New York 1955.

9. See J. Hick, *Evil and the God of Love*, Macmillan & Co., London 1966, Chapter XI and Harper & Row, New York 1966.

10. W. Golding, *The Inheritors*, Faber & Faber, London 1955.

11. C. Geertz, 'The Cerebral Savage' in *Encounter*, April 1967.

12. J. Hick, *op. cit.*, p. 320.

9

The Aspirant

The theme of *The Spire*[1] is the presence in even the noblest human aspiration of finitude and destructiveness. The story is set in mediaeval times. Its hero, Jocelin, is Dean of a cathedral. His understanding of his duties becomes concentrated into a single, consuming purpose – to add a great spire to the cathedral building.

> A new movement of my heart seemed to be building the church in me . . . so that in my new-found humility and new-found knowledge, a fountain burst up from me, up, out, through, up with flame and light . . . an implacable unstoppable glorious fountain of the spirit, a wild burning of me for Thee . . . The vision left me at last; and the memory of it . . . shaped itself to the spire, fitted into a shape; the centre of the book, the crown, the ultimate prayer (p. 193).

Jocelin has here described an experience which is not rare among men: the disclosure of a task which makes an ultimate demand and for which the visionary feels himself to be divinely appointed. 'And from that moment I knew why God had brought me here, his unworthy servant . . .' Jocelin is a chosen man with a specific work to do, and the work comes before everything. He is sustained by his sense of election through the immense difficulties of the spire's building.

Had the original builders of the cathedral intended it to have a spire? Jocelin thinks so, though there are no plans to prove it. But when a pit is dug at the crossing of nave and transepts above which the spire will be raised, the foundations are seen to be little more than enough to bear the weight of the existing building; and the four pillars which support the central part of the roof, although they seem immensely thick at eye-level, are thin in relation to their great height; moreover, they are not solid stone but stone shells filled with rubble.

At this point begins the conflict between faith and reason, between aspiration and practicality, between the vision of the spirit and the limitations of matter. Jocelin is the man of faith, vision, aspiration: Roger Mason, the master-builder, is the man of reason, practicality, knowledge. For Jocelin, nothing is impossible when there is faith because the work is God's work, not man's. For Roger Mason, faith becomes madness, a work of the devil, when it goes counter to technical expertise.

The claims of faith are set out with overwhelming conviction by Jocelin. The spire is not Jocelin's Folly, as people are now calling it, but God's Folly.

> Even in the old days he never asked men to do what was reasonable. They can do that for themselves. They can buy and sell, heal and govern. But then out of some deep place comes the command to do what makes no sense at all – to build a ship on dry land; to sit among the dunghills; to marry a whore; to set their son on the altar of sacrifice. Then, if men have faith, a new thing comes (p. 121).

That is a splendid assertion, the truth of which is not confined to 'religion' in a narrow sense. It bears witness to the transcendence of man, the reach which dares to stretch beyond the immediate grasp, refusing to be bound by rational calculation, risking the absurd.

But the counter-argument is put, with almost equal conviction, by the master-builder. It is he who has to actualize the vision, he who has to transform faith into stone, wood, and iron, he who has to balance weight against strength, to invent new techniques, to control a profane army of workmen. And all this he must do in the knowledge, hard-won from experience of his craft, that the spire is a structural impossibility. The Dean dreams of a miracle of faith: the master-builder knows the bondage of law inherent in the shallowness of foundations and the weakness of stone.

By his authority, strength of will, and eloquence, Jocelin forces Roger Mason on against the judgment of his skill until the pillars sing and later bend under the strain of the weight above them. So far, the conflict has been between faith and reason. But now a deeper conflict begins: it is between faith and flesh.

Three other people are in the central area of the story. They are Roger Mason's wife, Rachel, and Pangall and his wife Goody. Pangall is a descendant of the builder of the cathedral, and his job in normal times is to maintain the fabric as his father and grandfather have done before him. He limps and he is impotent. He becomes the butt of the gang of men working on the spire, who imitate his lameness and mock at his impotence. Pangall's wife, Goody, is the Dean's god-daughter. She is sweet and self-effacing; she has never complained about her arranged marriage to an impotent man. Jocelin is aware that the building-work causes her distress: 'I suppose, after all, it must make some difference to us.' He does not know at this stage how terrible the difference will be.

Roger Mason and Goody Pangall fall in love. Jocelin notices their secret exchange of glances, but his moral indignation abates when he reflects that this illicit love will promote the building of the spire because it will keep the master-builder on the job.

As the building of the spire proceeds and the strain on the supporting pillars increases, so also the strain on the people increases. The growth of the spire is matched by another growth – a growth of human sexuality, of pain and hatred and irresistible life which seems to spring out of the earth, bodying forth in its rotten, adhesive fruit the corruption of the flesh. Already the earth has moved in a kind of travail under the weight of the spirit: it is as though a monstrous birth is being brought forth from the dark depths of life.

> Among the rubbish lying at the bottom of the pillar, he (Jocelin) saw there was a twig lying across his shoe, with a rotten berry that clung obscenely to the leather. He scuffed his foot irritably . . . He had an instant vision of the spire warping and branching and sprouting (p. 95).

Woven through the work of faith is the growth of 'a plant with strange flowers and fruit, complex, twining, engulfing, destroying, strangling'. The plant, which exists only in Jocelin's imagination, is a symbol of elemental, chthonic reality disclosed suddenly in a glimpse of Goody Pangall.

Her hair had come out into the light. It hung down; on this side splayed over her breast in a tattered cloud of red; on that, in a tangled plait which doubled on itself, and draggled with green ribbon half-undone. Her hands clutched the pillar behind her, hip-high, and her belly shone about the slit of navel through the hand-torn gap in her dress (p. 90).

Faith is now in conflict with a more powerful contender than reason: the earth has moved in protest against the claims of heaven; spirit is challenged by flesh, transcendence by immanence, barren radiance by fecund darkness, wood, stone and iron by hair, blood and skin.

Jocelin tries to suppress flesh as he has suppressed reason.

However much he tried, he could not recreate the peaceful woman behind the hair . . . it was as if the red hair, sprung so unexpectedly from the decent covering of the wimple, had wounded all that time before, or erased it, or put a new thing in the way of the succession of days. So he would try to recreate the woman and the secure time, but find himself looking at the red hair instead (p. 91).

For a while, however, faith reasserts itself, vision is refocused, and dedication to the spire re-affirmed.

He shook himself for he felt her cling, and this was bad for the work. I must put aside all small things, he thought. If they are part of the cost, why so be it . . . I must climb away from all this confusion: I shall take this burning will of mine up the tower (p. 100).

Pangall (Goody's husband), tormented beyond endurance by the gibes of the workmen who mock his impotence, has by this time run away and Goody and Roger Mason have become lovers. But Jocelin has no time to spare for human tragedy. 'I can't pray for them, since my whole life has become one prayer of will, fused, built in.' It is the final betrayal of his religious duty: having abandoned responsibility for the cathedral services and works of charity, he has now repudiated his duty to his own god-daughter.

When Goody becomes pregnant, Jocelin's suppressed conscience reasserts itself and he tries to arrange for her admission to a convent. He goes to her cottage to tell her about this and

to give her money. He is met by Roger Mason being driven out
of the cottage by his furious wife. Jocelin enters the cottage
and finds Goody Pangall half kneeling. 'The light through the
door gleamed from her naked shoulders, and her head was
dropped, in a cascade of red, torn hair.' When she sees Jocelin,
her birth-pangs suddenly begin and she screams, short and
sharp, 'like the cruel blade of a knife'. Jocelin calls for help,
and the baby is born in a welter of blood which is like 'a
hideous ceremony of baptism'. Later that evening, when Jocelin
is praying, remembering his silent consent to the Goody-Roger
relationship for the sake of his own 'true love', the spire, he is
told that Goody Pangall is dead.

Work on the spire continues, but the cost of it in terms of
human flesh can no longer remain unacknowledged. Roger
Mason starts drinking; his wife, Rachel, fastens him to her as
with 'an invisible collar and chain'. Jocelin feels himself being
swallowed up by 'extraordinary tides of feeling': pictures of a
girl's feet, of her hair, her skin, her blood, rise up unbidden as
he tries to pray. 'The story . . . burned before his mind; and at
the crossways, the replaced paving-stones were hot to his feet
with all the fires of hell.' In the end, the spire is completed, but
Jocelin is removed from his deanship by the cathedral Visitor for
neglect of duty. Roger Mason becomes an incapable drunkard
and finishes up blind and dumb after an unsuccessful attempt
to hang himself. Jocelin dies of a painful disease of the spine.
His old cathedral colleague, Father Adam, ministers to him
and gives him the last Sacrament. Jocelin is an object of obloquy
to the people, and the spire is unsafe.

2

Golding's novel is rather like those tests for colour-blindness
in which a number has to be picked out from an area of variega-
ted colours. The complexity of the descriptions and the allusive-
ness of the writing make it difficult to 'spot the number', as it
were. But perhaps we may not be altogether mistaken if we think
of *The Spire* as Golding's version of the Tower of Babel.

The old myth in Genesis XI describes the collaboration of

all men in a mighty enterprise to build a tower which would reach up to heaven. Since the whole human race is involved, it is clear that the story is claiming to disclose a permanent truth about man's nature, the validity of which goes beyond merely local and historical conditions. The story draws our attention to the astonishing range of man's vision and the boundlessness of his self-confidence. There are no limits to the audacity of human enterprise: man has the power to transcend the limitations of his environment and his history; he seeks ultimate reality and absolute truth; he attempts to climb out of the relativism and finitude of his existence and to survey his condition from the standpoint of eternity. Here, precisely, is the grandeur and nobility of man, the interior vision and aspiration which refuses to be captured by the definition of environment. The men of Babel represent man at his most sublime, man at his very best, man in his distinctiveness from all other forms of sentient life.

Jocelin thinks of his spire in the same way as the men of Babel thought of their tower. He calls it 'the ultimate prayer' – the prayer which pierces every stage of prayer from the bottom to the top. The top of Jocelin's spire will be only 400 feet from the ground, but symbolically it will touch eternity, it will be equal with God. Human aspiration can go no further.

The men of Babel did not finish their tower. The Lord, we are told, came down and confounded their language so that they no longer understood one another and could not collaborate. No doubt this was an imaginative attempt to account for the puzzling fact that men do not all speak the same language, but perhaps we may take it in the general sense of inability to agree. Perhaps as the tower went higher there were quarrels about the design. Some may have doubted whether the foundations were deep and solid enough to bear the weight; others may have questioned whether the method of building with burnt brick instead of stone would give sufficient strength in high winds; others may have lost faith in the purpose of the enterprise, especially when the work became harder and more dangerous. No doubt there would be trouble with the labour-force: men may have been killed and injured; the danger and rigour of the work may have created psychological tensions leading to quarrels and violence. But the implication of the story is that the work stopped because man had overreached himself not in a physical but in a *spiritual* sense. There may have been a Jocelin at Babel whose faith in the enterprise was unshakable, but if there was he failed to convince the rest. The story of Babel reveals the central paradox of human nature: that man is aware of the Absolute but is himself inescapably relative; that he glimpses Eternity but is always a creature of time and place; that his noblest dreams are unattainable because he is man and not God. Thus it is not merely man at his worst who is aware of failure, but also – and far more significantly – man at his best.*

Jocelin's spire is built, but it is distorted and unsafe – a mere fragile symbol of man's infinite longing, witnessing to the inevitable imperfection of human achievement. Jocelin has claimed absolute truth for what is only a finite, temporary gesture; he has pretended to a finality which no human scheme, however inspired, can ever attain; he has believed himself to be the recipient of a unique revelation; he has forced the spire against reason and against flesh, convinced that he is doing God service.

In *The Spire* we have confirmation of the remark of Camus that when men believe that they are acting in the name of an Absolute, they quickly begin to regard *themselves* as absolutes and forget their inescapable contingency.[2] In their very attempts to actualize their visions, men fall into the pit and let loose destruction. It is this sense of non-attainment at the highest level of the human spirit that is the most important meaning of the doctrine of Original Sin. We do not really require a doctrine to tell us that man is prone to violence and barbarism, because that is only too obvious; what we do need is a doctrine which questions our noblest aims and reminds us of the mingling of evil with good in the best of our actions. Jocelin is told by Father

---

* See Reinhold Niebuhr's powerful essay 'The Tower of Babel' in *Beyond Tragedy*, James Nisbet, 1938. 'The higher the tower is built to escape unnecessary limitations of the human imagination, the more certain it will be to defy necessary and inevitable limitations . . . Human pride is greatest when it is based upon solid achievements; but the achievements are never great enough to justify its pretensions' (p. 29).

Adam that his prayer, of which the spire is both the product and the symbol, was 'a good prayer but not very good'. This expression – which belongs to the technical vocabulary of spirituality – means that Jocelin's prayer was partly acceptable to God but not wholly so, because it contained an element of self-regard and therefore belonged to the lower level of prayer at which the suppliant is not yet free from the downward drag of his sinful nature. The vision of the spire was like a reward given by a parent to a child – a spoonful of honey to encourage the child's efforts. But Jocelin has mistaken this low-level encouragement for absolute attainment, and has claimed the total endorsement by God of a finite and partly egotistic human project. The result is a *hubris*, a spiritual pride, which separates spirit from flesh and leads to a destructive denial of the springs of life.*

Jocelin's absolutist claims for his spire are falsified by the anguish of human flesh. The anguish of the flesh discovers the reality of the flesh both in the total scheme of things and in Jocelin's own consciousness. But Jocelin is a Manichean: he believes Goody Pangall to be a witch, an agent of the devil whose plan is to use Goody's sexuality in order to pollute the pure vision of the spirit. Goody represents all the messiness, the pain, the elemental tortured and rapturous life that binds man to earth and seems to drag down the spirit from heaven. It is Goody's loose, torn hair that constantly comes before Jocelin's inward eye, and its colour is the redness of blood – the violations of birth and death. The spire must now be understood as an attempt to escape from the pains and raptures of flesh into a state of spiritual beatitude from which flesh is excluded: it is a repudiation of the earth and a betrayal of responsibility for the sins of the world. The spire is therefore a lie, because it pretends that man can separate spirit from flesh and that God requires him to do so.

The irony is that the spire was itself made possible by the sins of the flesh. The money for it was supplied by Jocelin's aunt, Lady Alison, but she had obtained it from a lover who paid because her body pleased him and he wanted to give her a

---

* Cf. the remark of Camus, 'Virtue cannot separate itself from reality without becoming a principle of evil'. *The Rebel*, p. 263.

present. As Lady Alison says, it was she, not God, who chose
Jocelin for the work. Jocelin had asked the Bishop for money,
but all that the Bishop could give was a nail from the Cross.
Lady Alison is amused when she learns of this. The spire is not
pinned to the sky by the Nail, as Jocelin thinks it is : it owes its
very existence to the corruption of the flesh.

3

The question with which Jocelin wrestles is whether he is himself
infected. What kind of person was Goody Pangall? He had
watched her grow up and had loved her as a daughter, but the
vision of her which comes before his mind after her death
is of a very different person. She has become nakedly sexual.
What, then, is the relation of this vision to that other vision –
the spire? Is it a relation of enmity, of demonic against divine,
of appetite against obedience, of death against life? Jocelin
has a dream of her in the 'uncountry', the sphere of existence
where there is 'blue sky and light, consent and no sin'. He still
thinks of her as the devil, though her face is concealed by her
red hair. But she moves towards him, and then 'there was a wave
of ineffable good sweetness, wave after wave, an atonement'.
The grown woman is seen to be continuous with the innocent
child, and she comes to Jocelin now, with all hurt and conceal-
ment removed, as a reaffirmation of love.

But it is only in his dream that Jocelin sees Goody thus. In
his waking life he still does not know the truth about her. From
one point of view, he believes it was he who killed her because
he represented to her the Church's condemnation of her sin. Will
it ever be possible to heal the division between flesh and spirit?
Is there not, he wonders, 'some mode of life where one love
can't compete with another but adds to it'? Must sacred and
profane love always be at opposite poles, each demanding the
sacrifice of the other so that the being of man and woman is
torn apart?* Jocelin sacrificed Goody for the sake of the spire,
but she will not stay dead on its altar. She rises to bewitch him

---

* One is reminded here of the struggle between sacred and profane
love in André Gide's novel, *La Symphonie Pastorale*.

and to penetrate his dedication. Her red hair blinds his prayer, and the certainty of his divine appointment is subjected to a terrible questioning. On which side does truth lie?

The answer is given in the moment of clarity and freedom just before death.

> He looked up experimentally to see if at this late hour the witch-craft had left him; and there was a tangle of hair blazing among the stars; and the great club of his spire lifted towards it. That's all, he thought, that's the explanation if I had time: and he made a word for Father Adam.
> 'Berenice.'
> The smile became puzzled and anxious.
> 'Saint?' (p. 221.)

The Berenice referred to here was not a Christian saint but presumably the daughter of King Magas of Cyrene who married Ptolemy III, one of the Macedonian kings of Egypt. The significance of the name is found in the fact that Ptolemy called a star 'Berenice's curls' after his wife.* Goody Pangall has become 'Berenice' because Jocelin sees her red hair blazing among the stars. The vision means that Goody Pangall is on the God-ward side, that flesh is united with spirit and raised to the level of eternity. The spire no longer points away from the flesh but towards it, and the flesh, now redeemed from corruption, is seen to transcend the Manichean tower of the spirit. It may also be significant that 'Berenice' can mean 'bearer of victory'. Goody Pangall has been saved through the childbirth that killed her: she has been baptized in her own blood, and perhaps we are meant to understand that the sacrifice demanded of women by Nature is more acceptable with God than the trumped-up sacrifices invented by the spiritual pride of men. Goody is not, after all, a Circe, but a Beatrice, a bearer of that redemptive victory by which heaven and earth are reconciled.

Thus the liberation of man from futility and finitude comes, not through a Manichean denial of the earth, but through the

---

* Cf. Pope, *The Rape of the Lock*, Canto V lines 127-30.
  A sudden star it shot through liquid air,
  And drew behind a radiant trail of hair.
  Not Berenice's lock first rose so bright,
  The heavens bespangling with dishevell'd light.

uniting of earth with heaven. The shallowness of the foundations on which the spire is built makes the spire not only a physical but also a *spiritual* impossibility. Only if man is founded deep in the earth can he attain the life-enhancing fulfilment for which he strives. To be founded in the earth means to be a participant in the whole reality of human existence, including the struggle of its sexual, social and interpersonal becomingness, and to be alert to the hidden 'cellarage' of self-interest present in a man's mind. Golding seems to be telling us that transcendence comes *through* the earthiness of human reality, not apart from it. It is not Jocelin's spire but Goody Pangall's love that is endorsed by God, in spite of its paradoxical sinfulness. As Kenneth Cragg remarks of the divine intervention in the proposed sacrifice of Isaac by Abraham, 'it is when men believe themselves pursuing an absolute, whether perverse or plausible, that compassionate love is most urgent in its authority to interpose'. Goody Pangall's love is the love that interposes. There is no love for man in the spire – perhaps not even love for God. On the contrary, it crushes love and destroys those whose service it demands. Besides pointing out to us the egotism, the will-to-power which may be concealed in religious dedication, Golding reminds us that there is a lust of the spirit against the flesh as well as of the flesh against the spirit. Jocelin tries to climb away from the confusion of life: his spire is an escape route from the pain and travail of the flesh; it renders him impervious to human need and detaches him from human sin. But there is no redemption and no genuine enhancement of life in this separation of spirit from flesh. The flesh reasserts itself with life-affirming strength, and its symbol blazes among the stars.

With Goody Pangall, Golding almost seems to be making amends for what he did to Beatrice Ifor in *Free Fall*. The Jocelin-Goody relationship has much in common with the Sammy-Beatrice relationship. In both cases, idealization declines into exploitation and ends in collapse. We have already noticed how Beatrice fails to support Sammy's idealization of her, and how the relationship between them degenerates into one of sexual exploitation, concluding in the collapse of Beatrice into idiocy after Sammy's desertion. Just as Sammy idealizes the mystery of womanhood in Beatrice, so Jocelin idealizes the artless innocence of childhood in Goody Pangall and attempts to make her innocence permanent by marrying her to an impotent man. His Manichean attitude towards Goody is part of his motive in building the spire, and Goody's 'collapse' into sexuality is therefore seen by Jocelin as a threat to the spire itself. At this point, he repudiates her for the sake of his 'true love' and later thinks of her as an ally of the devil. But in his dream, Jocelin sees that Goody's sexuality is continuous with the joy and innocence of childhood : it belongs to the uncountry 'where there is no sin'. In Goody there is atonement, forgiveness, affirmation of the love which gives and suffers without exploiting. So far from being a human equivalent of the spire, Goody is its precise opposite. Therefore she gives the spire the lie. Against the exorbitant claims of a Manichean spirituality, she affirms the tragic worth of mundane existence.

4

Jocelin's spire is in a way comparable to Ralph's smoke-signal in *Lord of the Flies*. Both can be read as symbols of the human awareness of an order of existence outside our own from which 'salvation' may come. This belief and this hope go beyond reason and cannot be justified in terms of a closed, logical world. The smoke-signal and the spire are symbols of faith, of human aspiration refusing to accept the world as the final reality and reaching up to grasp a powerful rescuing hand. Essentially, this aspiration is religious, and is distinguishable from the pragmatic enterprise of discovering and mastering the physical order. Man finds it hard to suppress a sense that reality is greater than the area of his mastery and that his status is ultimately one, not of domination, but of dependence. It is possible for the sense of dependence to become so strong that the world loses any status as an order of reality and is devalued to zero or even to negativity. All value is funded into the supra-mundane. That is what happens in the case of Ralph and Jocelin, and I think Golding has given substance to the view which we noticed earlier – that the search for ultimate meaning diverts our attention from the alleviating labour which demands our action in the world, thus making us indifferent to human suffering. On this view, smoke-signals and spires represent a misdirection of energy away from the earth. If the world has at best only an instrumental value as a preparation for eternity, then there may be no reason for taking it seriously or for seeking to improve the condition of the people who inhabit it. Religious exercises and metaphysical inquiries trivialize secular values and entirely fail to help us to come to grips with our own reality as beings who are 'situated *there*', in the inescapable givenness of place and time. The worst state of all is when the conviction comes that absolute meaning has been found: what happens then is that men lose their sense of dependence and claim for themselves a quasi-divine authority. Ignazio Silone has given the political version of this.

> The deathly mechanism is always the same: every group or institution arises in defence of an ideal, with which it rapidly comes to identify itself, and for which it finally substitutes itself altogether, proclaiming its own interests as the supreme value. 'Whoever injures the Party is against History.' The members of the group in question are quite unruffled by this procedure; in fact, they find it serves their purpose.[3]

It is almost unnecessary to add that this 'deathly mechanism' operates in religion as well as politics. Silone could, with equal aptness, have said, 'Whoever injures the Church is against God.'

As we have seen, Jocelin absolutizes his vision of the spire and claims for it total value. Ordinary human existence is thus trivialized and even demonized when it resists the ultimate demand. The mundane order becomes at best a mere instrument of eternity or at worst of the devil. Those who cannot *see* this truth must, for their own good, be made to *serve* the truth, and Jocelin is the appointed authority to ensure that this is done.*

The opposite error to that of the devaluation of the secular order is its *over*-valuation and open hostility to the supra-mundane. Man may and often does refuse to acknowledge his dependence on a reality beyond his own area of mastery, and puts

---

* Cf. Sir Karl Popper's criticism of what he calls the doctrine that 'the Truth is Manifest', *Conjectures and Refutations*, Routledge & Kegan Paul, 1963.

himself forward as the dominating member of a closed world. 'Truth' then becomes identified with that which promotes the well-being of man in relation to the secular order, and is measured in terms of usefulness and power. Whatever increases control over the conditions of life is true; whatever lessens or subverts that control is false or meaningless.

The majority of the boys on the island repudiate the smoke-signal, the appeal to another order of existence, and turn to the enterprise of mastering their physical environment. In the excitement of the pig-hunt the fire is allowed to go out. But which is better – to spend one's time and energy in signalling to another world, or to hunt a pig and eat roast pork? The former enterprise looks to the future for a doubtful salvation; the latter ensures life-enhancing enjoyment now, the immediate reward of human effort. This latter view is plausible until Golding forces us to see its consequences. If the only values are those which promote power and usefulness, then the individual who fails to play his part in the power-game must be brought into subjection by power. There can be no place in this kind of society for the dreamer or the dissenter; nor can the existence of a rival group be tolerated. The energy and skill directed against the pigs is eventually directed against human beings, for the will-to-power will brook no restraint and can even justify murder.

When the divine is expelled, it tends to return in the form of the demonic, and as such may even be cherished. The supramundane order now appears, not as light and salvation, but as another and more powerful contender in the power-game whose presence is a threat to human domination. The 'beast' may even be cherished because it endorses the power-values which support the human struggle for mastery and so justifies violence and outrage. The only way of conquering the beast is to beat him at his own game. Anyone who says that the beast is not in fact bestial or who suggests that it does not exist at all runs the risk of being liquidated as a subverter of the values by which the human enterprise is sustained. Examples of this in our century are not hard to find.

What we require for our creative hazard is a relationship to the ultimate which neither disqualifies the mundane nor absolutizes human programmes. Man's empire over the natural order is not an autonomy snatched in defiance of a God who would disallow it, but a 'privilege' which belongs to the primal ordering of man in the world. The astonishing extension of the range of that empire in modern times does not pose any new problem about the relation of human to divine. Biblical faith does not discover God only in man's ignorance and weakness: it also recognizes his presence in man's knowledge and strength – in the very 'absence' of God there is a 'presence' which addresses man within the trust of his responsibility and freedom and calls him to account for his use of it. The human empire, when rightly understood, acknowledges that its domain is held under a greater empire which constitutes man both in his authority and his dependence and requires of him both venture and worship. It is only when man recognizes that his domain is thus held that he is both freed to meet its challenge and saved from his own destructive absolutisms.*

Notes

1. W. Golding, *The Spire*, Faber & Faber, London 1964 and Harcourt, Brace & World, New York 1964. The page references are to the Faber paperback edition of 1965.
2. A. Camus, *The Rebel*, Chapter V.
3. Ignazio Silone, 'The Choice of Comrades' in *Encounter*, December 1954.

* I am indebted in this paragraph to the chapter entitled 'Significant Absence and Real Presence' in Kenneth Cragg's *The Privilege of Man*, Athlone Press, London 1968.

Protest - Human and Divine

Professor D. M. MacKinnon has written that 'self-deception
. . . is one of the very deepest sources of the devastation which
evil brings into human life', and he adds in a footnote that 'it is
in literature that these things are often most clearly spelt out'.[1]
The survey attempted in this book supports MacKinnon's statement: it is precisely the self-deception of modern man that our
writers have sought to expose. For Sartre, deception is seen in
those who refuse the freedom to choose themselves and are thus
compelled to *appear* in order to *be*. For Camus, there is self-
deception in the belief that evil is an isolated external event, when
in fact it is the permanent absurdity of human existence itself.
Kafka presents the self-deception of those who think that their
existence can be justified by impersonal systems which offer
only circular definitions and never touch the substantial reality
of the individual. Golding shows us our self-deception when we
think that civilized values have altered our fundamental nature,
and when we claim an absolute status for what are, in reality,
self-regarding projects. We may risk the assertion that one reason
for the tragic sense of life is the fact that often we suspect that
we have deceived ourselves but do not know how until we discover the consequences of deception, by which time it is usually
too late. As Kierkegaard said, it is perfectly true that life must
be understood backwards, but we forget the other proposition,
that it must be lived forwards.* There is no way of knowing in
advance what the full outcome of our choices will be. The paradox is that we still know ourselves to be accountable for them,
and our authors are united in their repudiation of any self-
excusing views which would fasten blame on anything other
than ourselves. We are, in the vivid phrase of Sartre, 'condemned

* *Journal* 1843.

to be free'; to be human is to be accountable, but often we seem to have no access to the books until the balance has been struck. Our debts to humanity can then be read off in terms of the pain we have caused, the lies we have told, the injustice we have condoned; and there is neither God nor devil to blame for our bankruptcy. After almost two centuries of the rationalist hope, we have been forced to conclude that the final truth about Man is that his life is founded upon absurdity and contradiction.

In the face of the deep paradoxes in human awareness disclosed in modern literature, it should be obvious that there is little to be gained from either a shallow 'secularism' or a detached reassertion of traditional religious and moral formulas. Those of us who are attempting to preach the Gospel of Jesus Christ in the second half of the twentieth century may be tempted to greet pessimistic estimates of man with a shout of theological joy and start reaching for our sermon paper, convinced that we are in business again at last. This would be a mistake. There is a sense in which the denial of God is even more radical now than it was at the time of the Enlightenment. Man does not today say only in his mind, There is no God. He says it also in his heart (Unamuno). God cannot die; but as Nietzsche well understood, he can be murdered in the hearts of men. There are those today who think not only that religious belief is false but also that it is immoral and harmful because it claims to substitute, for the radical and paradoxical freedom of human existence, a ready-made and illusory supervention of meaning, which serves merely to conceal our responsibilities. On this view, the murder of God is the supreme act of justifiable 'homicide': it is the liberation of man from the prison of faith, the overthrow of the greatest deception in history. The result of this act may not be a recovery of health and happiness, but at least it leads to an honest assessment of the human condition and to the chance of a life freed from stultifying delusions.

This posture is, of course, heroic rather than pessimistic. The only real pessimism is the kind that despairs, not only of the Universe, but also of Man himself. We may assert that the Universe denies happiness and the triumph of moral good and the finality of personal love, but in our very act of setting out these denials we may be proclaiming our faith in the transcendence of Man. The grandeur of tragedy is to be found here – in the sense it gives us of man's superiority to a world which denies and destroys him. Any crushing event is popularly called 'tragic': a senseless accident, a broken relationship, a disappointed hope, mental or physical collapse. And these events *are* tragic because they force us to recognize the contradiction between what is and what ought to be, the fact that we live in a world in which the promise of life can be stunted and wasted by meaningless defeats. But to accept these defeats as the *final* truth of the Universe is to despair of *Man* and to fall into the only pessimism that really deserves the name. True pessimism comes when we *stop* saying *these things should not be*, when we not only expect disappointment but even allow our protest to become silent. Pessimism of this kind does not write books, does not defend itself, does not argue its case, for it is a withdrawal into the isolation of moral emptiness, the loss of transcendence.

2

In his study entitled 'Tragedy and Contemporary Ideas', Raymond Williams says that 'classical' tragedy is played out against a background of 'order' – of accepted beliefs or institutions against which the tragic-hero in some way sets himself. The effect of the tragedy, says Williams, is not merely to illustrate that order but to *recreate* it. The actions of the tragic-hero cause *dis*order – in a family, a State, the relation of human to divine – and the order which is finally affirmed, though it corresponds to the conventional beliefs which pre-exist the drama, is in fact recreated and made existential by the tragic action. The tragic events are thus related to a connected system of meanings, and the significance of suffering is seen in its power to revitalize those meanings.[2]

But modern tragedy presupposes *no* order of meanings, and it has been argued that genuine tragedy cannot now be written because there are no meanings to affirm. Suffering which leaves us in the absurdity where it found us merely affirms absurdity and cannot be redemptive because it fails to connect with any permanent values. If there is no source of meaning outside the self; if existence is gratuitous and unjustified; if human actions are subject to arbitrary forces which are themselves senseless – then there can be nothing but resignation to the Absurd and surrender of that human protest which is the core of tragedy. Life becomes a succession of accidents, and there are no rescue operations because man has abdicated.

We have noticed that Sartre does not altogether avoid leaving us in this condition – a condition which is in the end pitiable rather than tragic because there is no power to lift us out of it. There is no real protest inherent in the novels to which our own protest can attach itself, or else the form of protest is so bizarre that it leaves us unmoved. Sartre is right in thinking that there is no validity in a life which is supported by beliefs which have become mere evasions of responsibility, and in this sense it may be true that tragedy in the old manner cannot now be written. Yet it is extremely difficult to be a consistent absurdist, to reject steadily and with good nerves the alleged deceptions of faith and belief by which we seek to assure ourselves that our existence has a safe anchorage. Moreover, in this very determination not to be deceived there is discernible an integrity which must lead us to question absurdity as the final verdict, and it is merely arbitrary to suppose that such integrity does not resonate beyond the private world of the individual. We have noticed Heller's comment that the power to create the hostile world of Kafka must have its origin *outside* that world: there is a standpoint of meaning from which the verdict of absurdity is passed, and our very efforts to persuade others of the truth of this verdict imply that the standpoint is not a private one. To call the chessboard black is no less arbitrary than to call it white, though perhaps we should concede that Sartre and others are right in thinking that the latter option is the more damnable of the two. Christian faith should welcome a critique which forces faith back to its own Calvary and explodes its cheap complacency. Faith, as Thielicke says, is either a struggle or it is nothing.

Yet we may question whether 'despair' is the only alternative to 'bad faith'. Freedom without direction and without hope looks very much like another form of servitude: it is freedom *from* rather than freedom *for*, the power to grasp oneself in one's indeterminacy, one's radical independence of anything outside oneself by which one's being is defined. This is the state of 'despair' beyond which, as Sartre makes Orestes say in *The Flies*, human life begins. But it does not begin if there are no values to serve as criteria for our actions. It is not easy to distinguish the 'free' actions of the heroes of Sartre from the Romantic pursuit of self-realization. What seems to be missing is the shift from private to self-critical and altruistic attitudes – the only form of the human protest that is worth anything.

The contemporary complaint that life is meaningless cannot be met by exhortations to project oneself, to choose one's life, to decide autonomously what one shall be. We find 'meaning' in our lives, not by projecting ourselves into a void, but by aligning our endeavours with an order which we believe to be capable of endorsing them and incorporating them into its design. It is in this sense that the New Testament speaks of 'reward'. The kind of self-giving life commended and exemplified by Jesus will not finally be mocked and nullified by absurdity but will be confirmed and even transfigured by the resurrection victory in 'the rectifying future of God' (Moltmann). This is the 'reward' which energizes the Christian endeavour – the conviction that such endeavour is taken up into the divine Protest against destructive forces and will not spend itself in vain.

If it could be shown that it is possible to live affirmatively and creatively on the terms proposed by Sartre, then we would have to admit that the Christian estimate of man as one dependent on a source of meanings and values outside himself had been disqualified. But it is hard to think of any character in the novels of Sartre whose own life enhances the lives of those around him. The preoccupation of these persons with their own sense of dislocation seems to distort all their relationships, and we are left with puzzled individuals for whom the rich manifold of personal life has ceased to exist even as a possibility. What these excesses suggest to us is that the individual is incapable of creating his own reality. The time of death, as Eliot says, is every moment. It looks as if the Christian claim that the dislocation of the self requires the relocation of the self in the reality of God can now re-enter the debate.

Just as tragic drama is merely pathetic if it does not include within its substance a redeeming and recreating element, so also is our life pathetic if there is nothing to endorse our individual protest against evil. I do not believe that this is a battle which the individual can fight alone: a Sisyphean existence is unbearable – no man can live without the hope that some kind of apocalypse will finally vindicate and fulfil his labour, even if it is only winning the football pools. But there is more to this than endorsement of our *actions*: we also desire endorsement of *ourselves*, a sense that we are valued and affirmed for our own sake, not for the things we do. I think that Kafka is right here and that Sartre and Camus are wrong. The famous quarrel between the two French writers over the question of revolutionary violence in political action was not a fundamental divergence of view about the basic human condition: both were agreed that this condition was one of contradiction and absurdity. But Kafka's work represents a basic disagreement with Sartre and Camus in that it denies the possibility of wresting meaning out of the radical solitude of individual existence. All that the individual can do is either to build up his defences against intrusion and put his hands over his ears to shut out the hissing sound which spells their collapse; or else to recognize the unattainability of self-sufficiency and try to relate himself to some independent system. Kafka demonstrates the uselessness of positivistic systems for affirming the individual and making him feel at home in the universe, but I have argued that this need not be taken as a denial of all possibility of affirmation. The entrance to legal justification of the self may be barred, and the positivist heaven may be brass, but our task now is not to give up the search for meaning but to change the direction of our search while there is still time. Having eaten of the tree of *knowledge*, we must now eat of the tree of *life*.[3]

3

Kafka does not explain what he means by 'the tree of life'. Perhaps it was because his books stopped short at this point that he ordered them to be burnt. But obviously the tree of life symbolizes life in a much wider sense than that of biological existence. It points to a meaning which is in contrast with that of 'the tree of knowledge'. The realization that human knowledge does *not* give life is the central discovery of Kafka's heroes, and we may remind ourselves that the 'life' they are seeking is one in which the selfhood of the individual is related to and affirmed by an independent order of meanings and values. The human quest for 'life' in this sense is a right and necessary quest, but it is wrongly directed if it pins its hopes on an impersonal apparatus or any other system which separates a man from his comrades. The tree of life must therefore stand for the opposite of this: it must represent the reconciliation of man with his neighbour and the involvement of the individual in the despair and hope which all men share. Ultimately, we may venture to say, it must represent a source of affirmation which has its origin *outside* the human condition, and is not subject to the vicissitudes of mundane existence or the finitude and relativism of human history. It must stand as a permanent Protest against all that shuts up the individual in his self-created prison and denies the possibility of comradeship.

Kafka has of course drawn these two symbols of knowledge and life from the Genesis myth of the Fall, where the eating of the fruit of the trees is forbidden. After Adam and Eve have eaten of the tree of knowledge, they are driven from the Garden expressly in order that they may be *denied* access to the tree of life. But Kafka says that we are sinners, not only because we have eaten of the tree of knowledge, but also because we have *not yet* eaten of the tree of life. Man *has* eaten of the tree of knowledge and has discovered good and evil; he has also discovered that this knowledge does not enable him to penetrate to the heart of his own existence and to live creatively in a personal order which affirms him. What he needs above all is not a system of knowledge but an exit from the closed world of the self. This is presumably what Kafka means by eating of the tree of life. Man is to be saved, not by *gnosis*, but by his return to the Father's home.

This sense of *dependence* on a personal order is not the meaning of the tree of life symbol in the Genesis story. Here it stands not for dependence upon but for *equality with* God. It is a warning against self-deification. Man is shown to be firmly anchored in finitude and temporality: he has no access to the source of life and no possibility of lifting himself out of a condition which is characterized by unremitting labour and inescapable decline towards death. The existence of the tree of life and the denial of access to it are a permanent reminder of man's alienation from the eternal source of meanings and values. This biblical image is very like Kafka's picture of man as an exile whose very existence is marked by non-attainment and guilt. Kafka says that it is *necessary* to eat of the tree of life – the divine prohibition must be overcome if we are to avoid the surrender of the self to final despair. But the later use of the tree of life symbol in the Bible shows that it belongs, not to the sphere of human attainment, but to the sphere of divine grace. Prohibition of access will be lifted only when God in his forgiving and recreating mercy restores man to fellowship and brings him back from exile to the place where he is truly at home. Only if the giving of life is recognized as *divine* action can man be saved from destructive deification of himself.

4

In the New Testament, the tree of life symbol occurs only in the comparatively late book of Revelation.[4] In this context, of course, it is linked with the victory of Christ over sin and death and becomes available only through that victory. Because this book was written in a time of persecution of the Church, and has as its main intention the nerving of Christians to face a martyr's death, the symbol of life is placed on the other side of death where it overarches the river of the water of life which flows from the throne of God in the heavenly city. Only those are allowed access to the tree of life whose names are written in

the Lamb's book of life – those, that is, who have borne witness
to the Lordship of Christ over sin and death by offering themselves to him in martyrdom. But there is also the expectation that
the final triumph of Christ will be marked by the inclusion in
the heavenly city of all those elements in the human enterprise
which God can endorse and accept: the honour and glory of
the nations will be brought into the City of God. The leaves of
the tree of life will be 'for the healing of the nations', and men
will find fulfilment in the reign of love inaugurated by Christ.
We may recall the lines of Robert Browning:

> There shall never be one lost good! What was shall live as before;
> The evil is null, is nought, is silence implying sound;
> What was good shall be good, with, for evil, so much good more;
> On the earth the broken arcs; in the heaven a perfect round.
>
> All we have willed or hoped or dreamed of good shall exist;
> Not its semblance, but itself; no beauty, nor good, nor power
> Whose voice has gone forth, but each survives for the melodist
> When eternity affirms the conception of an hour.[5]

We do not hear so much today of this doctrine of 'the conser-
vation of values', as it used to be called.* It is certainly not among
the beliefs of the writers referred to in this book, and is indeed
at the opposite pole to that occupied by the Sisyphean heroes of
Camus. Against Camus I have tried to put forward the Christian belief that in Christ man has broken through absurdity.
The destiny of man is to share in the perfected humanness of
Christ, but this destiny does not lie, as Camus thinks it does, only
at the end of a long perspective which diverts our attention from
our historical existence. To use a metaphor from electronics,
there is a kind of 'feedback' from our destiny in Christ which
goes some way towards cleaning up our 'distortion', rather as
negative feedback cleans up the distortion in an amplifier
circuit. The knowledge that our human protest is taken up
into the Protest of Christ is what enables us to live hopefully
in an existence which is otherwise marked by Sisyphean non-

---

* E.g. T. E. Hulme, *Speculations*. The doctrine may also be said to
be present in Karl Barth's belief that the angels play Bach when praising God! He adds that among themselves they prefer Mozart, and God
likes to eavesdrop.

attainment. There is therefore a sense in which the tree of life is already accessible to those who seek to associate themselves with the self-giving of Christ and whose protest is not merely an act of grasping self-assertion. Our real choice lies, not between protest and submission as Camus claims, but between different kinds of protest.

The most suitable word for describing the Protest of Christ is *sacrifice*, and it is here above all that we have a criterion for assessing the true worth of the human protest. It would be false to say that every sacrifice has life-enhancing power. Raymond Williams rightly points out that everything depends upon the context in which the sacrifice occurs.[6] A man who dedicates himself to a personal ideal may very well sacrifice himself for it; but if his ideal works against the well-being, the freedom, the fulfilment of other people, then his sacrifice may be not merely worthless but even demonic. The human power of self-transcendence which astonishingly enables a man to give his life for the sake of an ideal may be disastrously misdirected if the ideal is itself destructive of human brotherhood. That is why the so-called 'supreme sacrifice' demanded by war is so ambiguous: valuation of the sacrifice must be related to the cause for which the war is being fought, and it is notorious that no cause of this kind can be endorsed unqualifiedly without a good deal of double-think. War is tragic, but there is a sense in which it does not become *tragedy* until its aftermath, when the human protest against death and destruction rises to repair the ravages and to re-assert the universal humanity of man which war has denied. The damnable fact is that man seldom makes this protest until he has passed through an experience of slaughter and destruction and learnt to abhor violation of life. That is what makes it impossible to shrug off Golding's *Lord of the Flies* as a mere 'fable'.

The life-enhancing purpose of Jesus is set out in the Fourth Gospel: 'I am come that they may have life and may have it in abundance.'[7] There are no limits to this purpose: the life Jesus brings is for all men and it is a liberation from every element in human existence which holds back the growth towards fullness. There is no question here of following an ideal which would devalue some men in order that others might be exalted, or of accepting a negation of some potentials in order that others might be realized. The work of Christ is universal in its range and inclusive in its dimensions: nothing human is alien to it – not even sin and death. The human context of Christ's sacrifice is nothing less than the totality of men and of all that they are capable of becoming.

The self-giving of Jesus is the divine-human Protest against the alienation of man from the springs of life. An important part of that Protest was directed against the distortion present in the physical order and the deprivation of life resulting from it. Jesus was concerned with poverty and disease; he was concerned with the selfishness which exploits human beings for personal advantage and with the righteous indifference which enables a man to ignore the suffering of others. He gave himself in his works of healing; on at least one occasion he fed the multitude; he refused to accept the traditional 'bourgeois' opinion that the poor and the sick *deserve* to be poor and sick; he challenged and loosened the stranglehold of the morality of merit and desert, and demanded love even for the thankless and evil. He went out into the wilderness to find the outcasts of society and he identified himself with their rejectedness in order to assure them of the welcome awaiting them in the Father's home.[8] His severest words were spoken to those who reckoned themselves to be righteous and despised others.

It is not the will of God that men and women should be crippled, diseased, blind, starving; nor is it the will of God that the riches of the earth should be inequitably divided. The action of Jesus in freeing men from slavery included their liberation from physical malfunctioning and insufficiency. This kind of liberation has been built into Christian obedience ever since, and is being undertaken with new though still far from adequate vigour today.* God in Christ has endorsed and immeasurably strengthened man's empire over the natural order, and it is right to include in that endorsement the validation of the scientific

---

* I am not claiming that this is exclusively Christian, of course. Much great and good work is done by those who prefer to call themselves 'humanists'.

and technological enterprise of our time while keeping steadily
in view the criteria of human need and enrichment by which
the enterprise must always be most urgently evaluated. 'Greater
things than these shall he do,' said Jesus,[9] referring to his own
works of healing and relief which have been multiplied thous-
ands-fold by modern discoveries and techniques. As Harvey Cox
says,[10] it is the Church's job to flash to the world the message
that the God who frees slaves and summons men to maturity
is still in business. The saints and martyrs of the human race
include those who have striven to discover and apply scientific
truth, often at self-sacrificing cost, and have thereby lightened
the burden of existence. The charter for this enterprise was
given by Jesus Christ, who, to use the words of Camus, 'refused
to bow down to pestilences', and whose purpose was that all men
should have fullness of life.

5

There are many heroes, both in literature and in popular fiction,
who resemble Christ in their sacrificial struggle against life-
denying forces.* We have noticed the doctor, Rieux, in *The
Plague*, who fights the disease because, as he says, it is his job,
but who finds in this struggle that he is identified with suffering
humanity and that the real substance of his protest is love, without which the world is dead. I have argued that love is not a by-
product of the human rebellion, but that it is a precondition
of rebellion in the absence of which there would be no rebellion
at all. As Rieux himself says, we become weary of the prisons of
work and duty, and what we desire above all is 'a loved face,
the warmth and wonder of a loving heart'. In short, we desire
affirmation of our *selves*, not merely of our actions. It is fundamentally this affirmation of the self that enables us to surrender
that self to the claims of a suffering, threatening world. Surrender of the self is by no means the same thing as self-effacement:
surrender is the giving of the self, the effortful projection of the

---

* Even the 'private eye' of popular detective fiction may be presented
as a Christ-figure. See Raymond Chandler's fine essay 'The Simple Art
of Murder' in *Pearls are a Nuisance*, Penguin Books.

self in compassionate and creative service so that meanings and values may be revitalized. Our trouble is that we cannot project a self which is broken and imprisoned and doubtful of its own reality. We know that we are fearful of the creative hazard and prefer our selfish, solitary burrows. This is the state of soul-destroying solitary confinement which Christian religion uses the word 'sin' to describe. Jesus was sinless because he inhabited the largest liberty where the soul is inflexible and sure because its freedom is grounded in the certainty of God. The question for man is whether his broken, imprisoned, and doubtful self can be recreated and freed in order that he may become identified with Jesus in healing protest against denial and violation of life.*

I believe that love precedes action and is not merely a by-product of it. I also believe that the human protest requires an integrated and liberated selfhood as its source. I wish to say that love is the power which creates selfhood and that the self can be affirmed only if it participates in an affirming structure. As we have seen, many structures do not have this affirming power but tend rather to negate selfhood and depersonalize the individual. Many work-structures negate selfhood because those who belong to them feel that they belong only in a functional way. Functionally the individual can always be replaced by another individual equally capable of performing the same function. 'With varying force,' says Raymond Williams, 'many of us break through to the realization that the pattern of our public activity has, in the end, very little to do with our private desires.'[11] So it may be that our reluctance to get out of bed and go to work is not just laziness but a fear that we are losing our being. The fate of the vast majority of people in the work-a-day world is to discover that they are replaceable. Strikes and demarcation

---

* I find myself in disagreement with Moltmann (*Theology of Hope*, pp. 333-4) when he says that the identity and continuity of the individual are given by the call of God to join in working for the kingdom of God. I do not see how the self can be surrendered to the work of mission unless there already is a self capable of being surrendered. It is only when we are ontologically affirmed that we can become eschatologically directed. Of course I would agree that selfhood is fulfilled and perfected through involvement in the work of the coming kingdom.

disputes are often protests against replaceability, which is a threat not only to one's job but also to one's selfhood.

I cannot stand alone as a self-created individual, but neither can I be myself if someone else can be my total substitute. I am in despair when I cannot participate with others, and I am also in despair when others rob me of the autonomy of my own subjectivity. Both types of despair appear in modern literature – the former, for example, in Kafka, and the latter in Sartre. What I need is affirmation of my self and the power in turn to affirm others. The name of this affirming structure of selves is 'love', and it is this that is being actualized in the world through the resurrection of Jesus Christ from its origin in God.

In her book *Christ the Representative*,[12] Dorothee Sölle helps us to understand this structure of love by showing that it depends upon the possibility of *representation*. My identity is given when I am recognized, taken account of, by others; but my identity nevertheless remains distinct from this recognition and is not 'identical' with it. The dialectic of representation is not a kind of alternating current passing successively from positive to negative and then back again: it is rather an awareness that both poles are simultaneously 'occupied'. 'We experience representation,' says Dorothee Sölle, 'when we are dependent on another or on others, and when we bear responsibility for another or for others.' She emphasizes the danger of absolutizing either of these two aspects. A dependence which is not also willing to accept responsibility easily involves 'the reduction of the person to immaturity', while responsibility without dependence all too soon becomes undisguised tyranny.

The representation of me by someone else is always only partial and temporary: if it becomes total substitution, then obviously I have ceased to count because the other person has taken my place fully and permanently and I have become superfluous. In the structure of love, we are related to one another by dependence and responsibility, and no part of the structure can be substituted for another part. The structure is maintained by opposing tensions, and it petrifies into collectivism or collapses into atomism if an attempt is made to eliminate the tensions.

Of course the inadequacy of the metaphor contained in the

word 'structure' is revealed when we find ourselves thinking of human relationships in terms of a fixed state held in equilibrium, like a bridge or a building. In the structure of love there is a constant shifting of tensions and a constant modification of shape and density without which everything would go rigid and sterile and would cease to be personal. The structure of love is always characterized by becomingness, in the sense that the individual selves who compose it never find that they are totally coincident with the present but are always being urged forward into the future to attain greater fullness of life. But this power of becoming is not separable from the structure of love, and its goal does not lie outside the structure. If we abandon love and try to follow some isolated course of self-realization, we find that our selfhood disintegrates because there is no one to affirm it. The identity we seek reveals itself within the structure, and the structure must be capable of affirming and accepting my past as well as my present if I am to accept myself 'without repugnance' and so become 'cleansed of the sin of existing' and open to the future.[13]

My past can be accepted only if there is one who has experienced it with me, one who knows what it is like to be solitary and at odds, one who, in his own suffering, has represented me in mine. In many of the novels we have considered, there is no person of this kind. The failure of the heroes of Sartre lies here. They know that the puzzles and agonies of their individual existence cannot be alleviated by general formulas or prescriptive bromides; but they also know that there is no one in whom they can find understanding, there is no friend to share the burden of existence where its weight is felt in the hidden depths of being.* Similarly, in Kafka the hero is unrepresented: there is no one to take up his case, no one to act for him in a way that shows understanding of his personal travail; he is alone in a world which accuses him. Even sexual love fails to reach inner reality: the romantic dream of union has crumbled into dust, leaving the individual even more painfully conscious of his solitude.

* Mathieu's feeling of comradeship with the defeated soldiers in *Iron in the Soul* may be an exception to this.

6

The Christian belief and experience is that Christ knows me and represents me in depth, and that in him God accepts and affirms me without any need for deception or pretence on my part. The one person before whom I can never appear as a 'salaud' is Jesus Christ. This is part of the meaning of the Passion and of the New Testament emphasis upon Christ's participation in the effect of sin. The Epistle to the Hebrews makes much of the fact that Christ suffered 'outside the gate': just as the Old Testament sin-offering was burnt outside the camp because it had become unclean, so Christ died outside Jerusalem in the wilderness where he bore the reproach of our alienation from God and man.[14] Christ stands with us under the curse of Adam and the curse of Cain and the curse of Babel, participating in our loss of God, our loss of our brother, and our loss of the world. He experienced 'the death of God' and the devaluation of himself to zero. He accepted this as a Protest against it, willingly representing all men in their solitude and rejectedness because only so could the past be accepted and the present activated into love.

The love of God actualized for us in Christ has no place in it for deception, for pretending that man is easily set free from his own past. It is very hard to break the entail of the past, to share and forgive and affirm. Nietzsche knew how difficult it was:

> To redeem the past and to transform every 'It was' into 'I wanted it thus' – that alone do I call redemption. But the will is powerless against that which has been done – the will cannot will back-wards – it cannot break time and time's desire. 'That which was' is the stone that the human will cannot roll away.[15]

But what if the stone *can* be rolled away by a will not human but divine? What if the divine will, present in a human life, were to stand under the curse and say 'I willed it thus – *for myself*; willed it as an act of love so that the past might be redeemed'? Then indeed our burden of guilt might be removed and 'the dawn of a new future might shine'. For the cross of Christ transcends the order of justice. In terms of law, Christ is innocent; but in terms of love, in terms of his representation of man, he shares in our guilt, he accepts the entail of the past. There is only one way by which law and endless retribution can be transcended: it is the way that accepts the full rigour of the law's judgment, participating in the consequences of evil deeds, standing under the curse in the pain of both criminal and victim, and yet bringing to this deathly condition the liberating power of a love which reaches up out of despair, which shares in the condemnation but does not condemn, which wills that the evil deed fall on himself in order that he may redeem it. Thus the Protest against the forces of alienation begins with a willing involvement in the conditions they have produced. If such involvement is merely a pretence, or if the one so involved is in some special way protected from the full assault of evil, there can be no redemption.

To take an extreme case, is there any God who can dare to present himself as the saviour of a victim of a concentration camp? What kind of God would he have to be in order that he might address himself to such a victim without presumption? Would he not have to be a God who had himself shared in the despair and agony of the victim? a God who knew what it was like to be expendable, to be devalued to zero and to exist hopelessly in a darkened earth? If God merely looks down on man from the heights of transcendent Being, he *dare not* come face to face with the men and women and children whose lives have been outraged. But the God who, in the words of Bonhoeffer, 'lets himself be pushed out of the world on to the cross'[16] – he alone is the God who can help.*

But the participation of God in the tragic condition of man is not of itself sufficient to affirm and recreate humanity. The weakness and helplessness of God in the world is only one aspect of the divine presence, and it may be that the modern emphasis on this aspect is in some danger of giving us a God who is as much a victim of 'tragic destiny' as we are. He may become like someone who tries to rescue a drowning man and gets drowned himself. We are grateful for his sympathy and heroism, but would wish that he had been a better swimmer. How are we to

---

* Since this paragraph was written, it has been powerfully endorsed by Ulrich Simon in his remarkable book, *A Theology of Auschwitz*, Gollancz.

understand the *power* of God in the world? How are we to understand him as one who is *not* wholly absorbed into the human context? How are we to understand his otherness, his transcendence?

God's word to us in Christ is never a mere accommodation to human systems: it always includes a judgment on and a radical questioning of those systems. The dialectic of the divine-human encounter does not at all abate the holy otherness of God. The disclosure of God in Jesus Christ does not diminish but rather increases our sense of the mystery of divine Being. It is only in terms of arbitrary power – the power of the god from the machine – that God is weak in the world, and this is because the structure of love which it is his purpose to create is not an 'apparatus' but a community of persons. The power of God resides in his love. It is a mistake to think that God has to divest himself of power in order to love, just as it is a mistake to think that in becoming immanent he ceases to be transcendent. The transcendence of God is seen in his limitless power to identify himself with man and to love to the uttermost.

But man comes under pressure from this love, and to those who have entered the faith-relationship with Christ it is sometimes an overwhelming pressure. There is always in the divine love that which breaks into the closed world of our self-centredness and forces from us a confession of guilt and failure. Even our very best actions are not exempt from such confession, though it would seem that this fact has sometimes been more firmly grasped by the novelists of our time than by the theologians. The latter occasionally remind us of the castle which tells K that his job is progressing very nicely when he knows perfectly well that he has not even started. A wholly permissive God is a wholly ineffectual God, and love is enfeebled when it is understood as a mere endorsement of human programmes. Reinhold Niebuhr reminds us that 'the idea of a jealous God expresses a permanently valid sense of guilt in all human striving'. We have in our century been too ready to identify our partial insights with ultimate truth. Modern man, says Niebuhr, declares that religion 'is consciousness of our highest social values'. But nothing could be further from the truth. 'True religion is a profound uneasiness about our highest social values.'[17] This uneasiness is not, as some would have us believe, a groundless neurosis: it is a proper awareness of human finitude, a recognition that we are always in some degree pestiferous and cannot help doing one another harm.

The power of divine love frees man for participation in the structure of love: he is himself affirmed and is able to project his selfhood in acceptance of responsibility for others. There is no question here of forcing the individual into a prefabricated apparatus which deprives him of his freedom. As David Jenkins says, 'to be taken up by personal love which is expressed in terms of complete openness, identification and compassion to the point of irresistible union is not to be swallowed up but set free to be yourself, in union with God and with every other loved and loving self'.[18] When the human context is extended into the divine context in and through Jesus Christ, we see that our human protest against the forces of alienation is itself derived from the divine Protest, and that the freedom we claim is the freedom *of God* – the freedom which enables us to come out of our individualist prisons and to share in the divine self-giving. The kind of life to which this freedom leads will be far from being a comfortable state of rectitude: it will be marked by the cross, and those who enter it will find that 'the sorrows of the world are sorrow, and will not let them rest' (Keats). But it will also be a life of creativeness and hope, permeated by the Resurrection victory.

The four sculptures which Michelangelo did for the tomb of Pope Julius look unfinished.[19] The figures are emerging from the rough stone as though they were tearing themselves out of it with tremendous effort and pain, drawing towards an assertion of triumph which yet includes within it the agony of the creative protest. The Protest of Christ is like that: the new man is drawn out of the dereliction of the cross; he is liberated from the stone tomb of his isolated self to a resurrection which is not escape but victory, including within itself the pain over which it has triumphed. Yet this sculpture is also unfinished: its completion waits for us, for the revealing of the sons of God, in whom the liberating creative Protest is at work fashioning us to his likeness.

Stone can be the rock of Sisyphus, the burden of existence which we push up the mountain only to see it roll down again to the bottom; it can be the stone of Medusa's gaze which fixes us for ever in a petrified present; it can be the stone with which we build our precarious towers of Babel. But for the Christian the stone of human existence is the raw material out of which the masterpiece of God has been and is being created.

Notes

1. D. M. MacKinnon, 'Conceptions of Atonement' in *Prospect for Theology*, ed. Healey, James Nisbet, Welwyn Garden City 1966.

2. R. Williams, *Modern Tragedy*, Chatto & Windus, London 1966, p. 52 and Stanford University Press, 1966.

3. The reference for Kafka's cryptic remark about the Tree of Life is given by Moeller, *op. cit.*, Tome III, p. 229.

4. Revelation 22.2.

5. R. Browning, *Abt Vogler*.

6. R. Williams, *op. cit.*, pp. 156-7.

7. John 10.10.

8. Cf. H. A. Williams, *The True Wilderness*, Constable & Co., London 1965 and J. B. Lippincott Co., Philadelphia 1965.

9. John 14.12.

10. Harvey E. Cox, *The Secular City*, SCM Press, London and The Macmillan Co., New York 1965, p. 127, and Penguin Books, 1968.

11. R. Williams, *The Long Revolution*, Chatto & Windus, London 1961, p. 106 and Harper & Row, New York 1966.

12. D. Sölle, *Christ the Representative*, SCM Press, London 1967, p. 56.

13. The quotations are from Sartre's *Nausea*.

14. Hebrews 13.11-13.

15. F. Nietzsche, *Zarathustra* – 'Of Redemption'.

16. D. Bonhoeffer, *Letters and Papers from Prison*, SCM Press, London, Revised ed. 1967, p. 196 and The Macmillan Co., New York.

17. R. Niebuhr, *Beyond Tragedy*, James Nisbet, Welwyn Garden City 1938, p. 28 and Charles Scribner's Sons, New York 1938.

18. David E. Jenkins, *The Glory of Man*, SCM Press, London 1967, p. 110 and Charles Scribner's Sons, New York.

19. *The Four Captives from the Boboli Gardens*, Accademia di Belle Arte, Florence.

Bibliographical Note

In addition to the books mentioned in the text and notes, I wish to acknowledge indebtedness to the following:

Literary

R.-M. Albérès, *Jean-Paul Sartre*, Editions Universitaires, Paris 1953

G. Brée (ed.), *Camus, a Collection of Critical Essays*, Prentice-Hall, New Jersey 1962

Flores and Swander (ed.), *Franz Kafka Today*, University of Wisconsin Press, 1962

W. Hubben, *Dostoevsky, Kierkegaard, Nietzsche and Kafka*, Collier Books, New York 1962

Komey and Mphahlele (ed.), *Modern African Stories*, Faber & Faber, London 1964

C. S. Lewis, *The Allegory of Love: A Study in Mediaeval Tradition*, Oxford University Press, London and New York 1936

R. de Luppé, *Albert Camus*, Editions Universitaires, Paris 1952

Moore and Beier (ed.), *Modern Poetry from Africa*, Penguin Books 1963

Philosophical

D. G. Charlton, *Positivist Thought in France During the Second Empire*, Oxford University Press, London and New York 1959

K. Jaspers, *Reason and Anti-Reason in our Time*, SCM Press, London 1952 and Yale University Press, 1952

C. Smith, *Contemporary French Philosophy*, Methuen & Co., London 1964 and Barnes & Noble, New York 1964

Wahlens and Biemel, Introduction to Heidegger's *De l'Essence de la Vérité*

Theological

R. Gregor Smith, *Secular Christianity*, Collins, London 1966

J. Macquarrie, *An Existentialist Theology*, SCM Press, London 1955 and Harper & Row, New York

J. Macquarrie, *Principles of Christian Theology*, SCM Press, London 1966 and Charles Scribner's Sons, New York

P. Tillich, *The Courage to Be*, James Nisbet, Welwyn Garden City 1953 and Yale University Press, 1952

P. Tillich, *Love, Power and Justice*, Oxford University Press, London and New York 1954

A. R. Vidler (ed.), *Soundings*, esp. essays by H. E. Root and H. W. Montefiore, Cambridge University Press, Cambridge and New York 1962

Ethical

K. Jones, *The Compassionate Society*, SPCK, London 1966

L. Hodgson, *Sex and Christian Freedom*, SCM Press, London 1967 and Seabury Press, New York

Sex and Morality, A report presented to the BCC, SCM Press, London 1966 and Fortress Press, Philadelphia 1966

H. Thielicke, *The Ethics of Sex*, James Clarke, London 1964 and Harper & Row, New York 1964

General

Jacques Choron, *Death in Western Thought*, Collier Books, New York 1963

Index